Wake up...
Live the Life You Love, Living on Purpose

Other books By Steven E

1994
Wake Up
An Inspirational Handbook

2001
Wake Up...Live the Life You Love
(1ˢᵗ Edition)

2002
Wake Up...Live the Life You Love
(2ⁿᵈ Edition)

2003
Wake Up...Shape Up...
Live the Life You Love

2003
Wake Up...Live the Life You Love:
Inspirational "How to" Stories

2004
Wake Up...Live the Life You Love in Beauty

For your free gift, go to: **www.wakeupgift.com**

Wake up... Live the Life You Love, Living on Purpose

Wake up...
Live the Life You Love,
Living on Purpose

By
Steven E
&
Lee Beard
and 45 coauthors

Published by:
Little Seed Publishing, LLC.
P.O. Box 4483
Laguna Beach, CA 92652

COPYRIGHT © 2004 by Global Partnership, LLC

Pre-Press Management by TAE Marketing Consultations
Robert Valentine, Senior Editor;
Katie Dunman, Associate Editor; Adam Mathis, Assistant Editor;
Jennie Crawford, Editorial Assistant;
Erin Forte-Wilson, Associate Editor and Public Relations
Text Design: Wm. Gross Magee

Cover Design: Klansee Bell

For information, contact Little Seed Publishing,
P.O. Box 4483, Laguna Beach, CA 92652, or phone 562-884-0062.

Distributed by Seven Locks Press
3100 W. Warner Ave. #8
Santa Ana, CA 92704

Library of Congress Cataloguing-In-Publication Data
ISBN: 0-96447-6-7
$14.95 USA $24.95 Canada

For your free gift, go to: **www.wakeupgift.com**

DEDICATION

*O*ur history is resplendent with the deeds of those who could not be swayed from their goal. The firmness of purpose in these individuals helped give them a path to walk on and enabled them to walk it.

Let us dedicate ourselves to finding a purpose for which it is worth dying and living.

This book is dedicated to such people, both who still search for, and those who have found, their purpose.

Steven E and Lee Beard

Wake up... Live the Life You Love, Living on Purpose

Contents

Wake up... Live the Life You Love, Living on Purpose

Purpose in Life

Steven E

We all have a purpose in life. You have a unique talent and personality that nobody else has. Think of something you love to do and figure out how to make a living doing it. When your life is in working order, your whole existence is so much easier.

If you are currently in a job you do not like, take time to work on the things you enjoy and set a patient timetable for making these changes.

If you do not know what your purpose may be, sit quietly and go within, asking for the answer. All of the answers are within you. Purpose defines us. Think of the things you like to do that brighten your day and make you smile—things you would do for no money but just for the enjoyment. I am urging you to go do it, and not to give up on your vision. We only live once, so do what you love to do. Find your purpose in life and work with a smile. You have a gift to share with the world. Do not be selfish but share your purpose and gifts doing something in which you believe. The world deserves it, and so do you.

Finding your purpose in life is recognizing that you can start being "on purpose" in this moment, because being "on purpose" is about loving unconditionally and serving others. Start now and follow your interests, even if you know that your career or life situations will have to change. Focus your thoughts and intentions on loving and serving other people.

Learn to make giving more important than receiving because giving is in alignment with your purpose. No one has to tell you when you are "on purpose;" when you find your passion in life and you move forward with an unstoppable drive. You no longer question the meaning of your life. Everything you do is synchronized with your higher self. You fulfill people and feel fulfilled from your actions.

When we are born into this world, we arrive with no material items and leave just as empty-handed. We can't take any material items with us. The message of your life is to give. Learn to give unconditionally and live a life that you love.

Steven E
Creator of the number one best selling series,
Wake Up ... Live the Life You Love
www.wakeuplive.com

Conceptualizing Your Purpose

Mark Victor Hansen

No one ever succeeds without a clear grasp of purpose. When you look at the lives of the most successful people who ever lived, you can see that they had a definite purpose and knew it.

Christ's purpose was spiritual and was stated in John 10:10: "...I am come that you might have life, and that you may have it more abundantly."

Walt Disney's purpose: "To make people happy."

Andrew Carnegie's purpose: "To manufacture and market steel."

Mother Teresa's purpose: "To care for and comfort the poor, sick and needy all over the world."

What is your purpose? You cannot find the answer in a book or a class, but would it not be fantastic if you could? The answer can only be found deep inside of you.

How do you find your purpose? My suggestion is meditation or deep, controlled, concentrated thought. Find a quiet place where you won't be disturbed. Relax and tap into your mind, back there in the deepest, secret compartment of your mind by asking yourself, "If I knew my life's purpose, what would it be?"

Don't just ask it once. Keep asking this question until you get the answer. It may not come on the first day, or even the first week. But it is there, and it will show itself if you earnestly ask. Your constant and sincere question is like a beacon that will draw your purpose to your consciousness and show it to you clearly illuminated.

Meditate on your purpose every morning and every night for 15 minutes until the answer comes to you. Then, be sure to write it down. Don't be surprised if it comes to you during the day while you are exercising, while you're at the grocery store or taking the dog for a walk. Be open to the answer, no matter when it comes to you.

Remember, your purpose is the deepest expression of yourself. In a way, it wants you just as much as you want to know your purpose in life.

Let us hear from you.

Mark Victor Hansen

Embrace Silence

Dr. Wayne Dyer

You live in a noisy world, constantly bombarded with loud music, sirens, construction equipment, jet airplanes, rumbling trucks, leaf blowers, lawn mowers and tree cutters. These manmade, unnatural sounds invade your sense and keep silence at bay.

In fact, you've been raised in a culture that not only eschews silence but is terrified of it. The car radio must always be on, and any pause in conversation is a moment of embarrassment that most people quickly fill with chatter. For many, being alone in silence is pure torture.

The famous scientist Blaise Pascal observed, "All man's miseries derive from not being able to sit quietly in a room alone."

With practice, you can become aware that there's a momentary silence in the space between your thoughts. In this silent space, you'll find the peace that you crave in your daily life. You'll never know that peace if you don't have any spaces between your thoughts.

The average person is said to have 60,000 separate thoughts daily. With so many thoughts, there are almost no gaps. If you could reduce that number by half, you would open up an entire world of possibilities for yourself. For it is when you merge in the silence, and become one with it, that you reconnect to your source and know the peacefulness that some call God. It is stated beautifully in Psalms of the Old Testament, "Be still and know that I am God." The key words are "still" and "know."

"Still" actually means "silence." Mother Teresa described the silence and its relationship to God by saying, "God is the friend of Silence. See how nature (trees, grass) grows in silence; see the stars, the moon and the sun—how they move in silence. We need silence to be able to touch souls." This includes your soul.

It's really the space between the notes that makes the music you enjoy so much. Without the spaces, all you would have is one continuous, noisy note. Everything that's created comes out of silence. Your thoughts emerge from the nothingness of silence. Your words come out of this void. Your very essence emerged from emptiness.

All creativity requires some stillness. Your sense of inner peace depends on spending some of your life energy in silence to recharge your batteries, remove tension and anxiety, thus reacquainting you with the joy of knowing God and feeling closer to all of humanity. Silence reduces fatigue and allows you to experience your own creative juices.

The second word in the Old Testament observation, "know," refers to making your personal and conscious contact with God. To know God is to banish doubt and become independent of others' definitions and descriptions of God. Instead, you have your own personal knowing. And, as Meville reminded us so poignantly, "God's one and only voice is silence."

Dr. Wayne Dyer

People Are Starving
R. Winn Henderson, M.D.

Growing up during the early 60s, I wanted to share with the less fortunate in the world. I did this by donating money made by cutting the yard to help support and feed a little child from South America. By the time this child was old enough to be off the program, I too had grown up. Medical school, marriage and a new career consumed most of my time.

Through my medical practice, I donated time to treat those who had no insurance and no way to pay. This was now my way of giving to others. The plight of hunger had been put on hold. It is so easy to get caught up with our own lives that we completely forget about the people who need our help the most.

In my fifties, what seemed important in my thirties and forties no longer mattered. My focus came full circle to when I was as a grade school boy with a burning desire to help the hungry children in the world. God put this burden on my heart, and since then I have done everything within my power to do something about feeding these children. I wrote a book that explains how a person can take excess weight from his or her own body and transfer it to hungry or starving people in the world. No surgery is involved. Only a small mental sacrifice on our part is required.

Do we continue to fuel our bodies with food we don't really need, or do we use this asset to feed someone in the world who is hungry or even starving to death? When you think about it for just one second, the answer is clear.

We were not put here to constantly indulge ourselves. God fully expects each and every one of us to reach out to help the less fortunate.

Find out how I discovered this truth. I share my personal transformation on page 119 of *Wake Up And Live The Life You Love,* 3rd Edition.

If the TV commercials that picture starving families all over the world pull on your heart strings, please do something about these feelings. Hunger exists in every country including our own. This is not because the hungry person is lazy, but simple due to the conditions these people were born. They simply have no money to buy food.

An E-book copy of *The Sacrifice Diet,* which explains the whole process of how to transfer weight you don't want to someone who needs it to survive, is available to you free of charge. Just e-mail me at drhenderson7@mchsi.com and put *Free Book-Wake Up* on the subject line.

Feeding the hungry does not guarantee you a crown in heaven, but it will provide you with joy, happiness and peace of mind. The most we can hope for when we reach Heaven is a pat on the back and to hear the words, "My child, well done!"

R. Winn Henderson, M.D.
drhenderson7@mchsi.com
828-586-0094

Purpose and Faith Smooth Out
the Roller Coaster of Life

Carolyn K. Perry

*I*t is exciting to see a baby try repeatedly to stand and then to walk, often toward a loved one. The child's eyes gleam with joy and there is no evidence of distress at the many falls needed to achieve the happy moment. A sense of purpose has carried them past those falls to success.

As a child, the love and approval of my family and the desire to make them happy by being successful was very important to me. It cushioned the harshness I experienced from a lack of new clothes, cruel comments made by my peers about my attire and one teacher's occasional derogatory remarks about my living in the country. Luckily, my dad went to bat for me and the teacher stopped her negative statements about me. By the end of the school year, I had the best grades in the class. Unfortunately, the cushion I relied on from my family came tumbling down when my parents were separated and then divorced.

In response to this turmoil, I got involved in school organizations and joined a young people's group at church. In these groups, I found friends with goals and faith for the future. I internalized the belief that I would go to college even though I had no clue from where the money would come. With sacrifice, each of my parents contributed a total amount covering a half of the cost for each year. I worked summers and had a small grant allowing me to complete all requirements in seven semesters of college.

I had to start work immediately after graduation, even though I really wanted to go to medical school. Just as I was about to get the chance to go to medical school, I met the man who would become my husband of 23 years. I chose to resume my career in medical technology, which was more compatible with marriage at that time. As it turned out, not getting into medical school was a blessing.

Continual learning propelled me to a knowledge level which allowed me to present a case study at a national meeting. It also enabled me to earn Hematologist and Special Hematologist registrations from the American Society of Clinical Pathologists. Best of all, I was able to help many people.

I started working on my MBA and was more than half-way through, when my husband was diagnosed with cancer. There was only one choice. He was more important than the MBA.

My daughter came home from college and took the afternoon shift after the hospice worker left and before I returned from work at the hospital. What a blessing! The hospice people were so helpful that even while my husband was still alive, I vowed to help the cause as soon as I was able. The thought of helping others eased the pain of my loss a few weeks later.

In fact, my faith helped me to understand the pain suffered by my teen-aged son, who had also lost his best friend. I realized I needed to be strong for him. I also needed to be strong to fight in court for five years for the correct pension amount from my husband's account. With the help of an expert lawyer and my faith, purpose and truth won again. Near the end of this ordeal, I started a financial services business part-time. God never stopped giving me strength.

But soon, I faced an incredible personal challenge. My right arm had deteriorated completely, following an ergonomic injury and for three years, my arm was basically useless. Early on I begged God to carry me, because I had no earthly strength left. After two necessary surgeries and with continued faith, I found a doctor who believed my arm would be healed – with some massage therapy. Although, I could have wished for a faster timetable to recovery, my arm is functioning again at greater than 80 percent.

God is good, and now I have another purpose in addition to helping businesses with their cash flow, helping hospice and watching proudly as my children find their way in life. My purpose is centered around ergonomic research, education and treatment and general wellness empowerment.

I have no idea how many other ups and downs life has in store for me, but I know no matter what comes along, reaching out to others and to whatever higher being a person acknowledges is the surest cure to the extremes of the roller coaster of life.

Carolyn K. Perry

It's time to wake up and live the life you love!

Sian Buckley

Twelve and a half years ago, I lived with my family in a small, three bed-room house. I was working an 8-to-5 job as a branch manager for a large corporation. I earned an above-average salary and was bored out of my mind. Something had to change. I had to change.

I did some soul-searching and realized that freedom was my number one priority. There was no external expression of this in my life. I wanted the freedom to work the hours that suited me. I wanted the freedom to write my own check. I wanted to feel excited and passionate about the work in which I was involved. I wanted to be there when my children came home from school. I wanted to gain personal and financial knowl-edge to enjoy a relaxed and peaceful lifestyle.

I started reading self-development books by self-made millionaires. I read all the financial literature I could get my hands on. I learned that one way to achieve true financial success was to put a plan in place to build assets, like businesses and properties, and earn passive income.

I examined my history, looking at the way my parents had managed money and how I acted out my habitual beliefs and behaviours. I wrote down what I enjoyed doing as a child. My sisters, Rosemary and Jennifer, reminded me of my entrepreneurial activities. When I was eight years old, I used to buy boxes of sweets. I would work out how many cups there were in each box, double the price and make a profit selling them to the children at school. There were numerous stories of my moneymaking activities as a child.

As a child, I seemed naturally interested in business and money. So after much soul-searching and with a huge leap of faith, I took the first big step and left my "secure" job to start my own business in the financial planning industry.

At first, I was afraid, but I decided that success was the only option and I would accept nothing less. I had financial commitments that I had to meet every month so I had to be successful. I also knew that in order to master money and achieve both personal and financial success, I would first need to overcome my fears and challenge my personal comfort zone.

I have gained great knowledge and experience over the past twelve years. It has not all been smooth sailing. My husband, Jonathan, and I have built five businesses from scratch and sold two that were too time-consuming. In 1994, we bought our first two investment properties. It was very stressful the first time we entered the property market, as this was a huge step for us. Once we became comfortable with renting the first two properties, we continued to buy more. We have bought twelve investment properties in the past ten years and we plan to buy another eight in the next five years.

We have had highs, lows and serious challenges in our businesses and family life. Our son, Darren, became a quadriplegic at the age of 18 years old, when he broke his neck in a diving accident. Darren is now coping well with his life-changing situation and it took our family a year to come to terms with this tragedy. Life can be fragile. There is no time like the present to live every day in the best and happiest way that we can.

We don't have control over external circumstances and life sometimes throws a wobbly at us, but the human spirit is strong and we can always find the strength and support to bounce back from these painful experiences.

I have found my passion and I love what I do. It doesn't feel like work. I am a co-director of a company called Astron Money Managers in South Africa. We help people to turn their lives around and use our accredited certified programmes to show them how to manage their own money and find the freedom and money to be, do and have more.

Today, I have the freedom to work the hours that suit me, to write my own check and to stay at home with my family when I choose to, and every day I continue to learn and gain personal and financial growth. I have the freedom to be me. You too can have the freedom to be you!

Sian Buckley

Surfing and the High Wire
Ralph McCutcheon

*H*ave you ever noticed that life seems to be a series of ups and downs? "More downs than ups," many would say. Creation is based on the principle of duality, so as well as down and up, we have in and out, back and front, happy and sad, loving and hating. Everything has its equal and opposite—the Yin and Yang of Chinese philosophy.

As individuals, we can choose which side we want to be on: positive or negative, optimistic or pessimistic, loving or hating, creative or destructive. We are a bit of each, but our root desire is set firmly to the positive, creative and loving experience of life.

What gets in the way of our desire? We find all sorts of excuses for making life hard for ourselves! Life is hard; people are mean; "They" never do enough; there isn't enough; I could never do that; they are so lucky, etc.

The answer is in ourselves, never in others. In most societies we are programmed from birth to see the threatening side of life, and this becomes the default program on our internal computer. 'What if' is a sensible, responsible position according to our parents, who want to protect us from the consequences of rash actions. However, preoccupation with the negative possibilities can make us over-cautious, suspicious and pessimistic.

Life for a human is a bit like walking a tightrope. We have to keep our balance and fall neither to one side or the other as we inch our way carefully along the high wire to the other end. We could say that a fall to one side was 'good' and a fall to the other side was 'bad,' but really it is just a fall from that tightrope. So we pick ourselves out of the ever-present safety net, climb up and start again.

We gradually wobble a bit less often and with more grace, and learn to rejoin the rope from where we fell rather than going right back to the beginning again. We discover that carrying the balance pole of faith and belief helps tremendously, and we edge forward more confidently.

And then the lights go out! Someone is playing around, just as we are getting our act together! We are suddenly feeling alone, disoriented, terrified. We can't be sure the safety net is still there. So either we panic or stop, losing our grip on the pole of faith and belief and fall, or we keep our eyes set firmly on our destination, don't look down, keep a firm grip on our pole and continue slowly until we can see the way again.

Gradually, as we inch along the rope of life, we become more adept, more poised, swing less from side to side; from meanness to generosity, from love to fear, from joy to depression, from shyness to boastfulness. We find that balance is the one thing that keeps us on our journey.

And so we become more and more skilful, to the point where we can perhaps call across to others on their own journey with some basic hints. The most important encouragement is to never look down and keep your sights firmly on your destination. Sometimes we can signal a timely reminder that there is always a safety net down there somewhere.

So, to use another metaphor, once we have a good sense of balance we can progress to all sorts of other exciting things. Even tightrope walking becomes boring after a while! So what about going to Maui to do a bit of surfing? Seeing those guys tackle the highest waves and ride them is exhilarating, but just imagine the excitement of doing it yourself. Even perhaps getting into the tube of a curling wave and surfing faster and faster toward the inevitable breaking of the wave and its dissolution on the beach, and your adrenalin high as you realise you have survived life at the extreme edge.

I have fallen countless times on my way to developing balance and conquering the fear of falling. What a blast! The wave does nearly all the work, just so long as I don't try and fight it. The sun keeps shining, and I play along the crest. But I dare not drop my awareness for a split second or I will be engulfed and have to half-drown, recover and find another wave. Fortunately, I have developed a sixth sense for impending trouble; it effortlessly saves me time and again just so long as I trust it, allowing me to relax into savouring the continuing thrill of being truly alive.

Ralph McCutcheon

Why Am I Here?

Deepak Chopra

From an Interview with Dr. R. Winn Henderson

*T*he majority of people on earth are unfulfilled or unhappy because they do not have a purpose or a mission. As a part of the human species, we seek purpose and meaning; we laugh, and we are aware of our mortality (that one day we will die). This is what distinguishes us from other creatures. Laugher, mortality and purpose become three important, crucial questions. We search for meaning – a deep significance to life.

Why am I here? Why have I been placed on the earth? We've been placed on earth to make a difference in life itself and in others' lives. In order to make a difference, we must find what we are good at, like to do and benefits others.

We all have a mission, and my mission in life is to understand and explore consciousness and its various expression and also to share that with anyone who's interested in doing the same. It boils down to understanding the mechanics of healing, the rule of love. I would say to put it very simply, my mission is to love, to heal, to serve and to begin the process of transforming both for myself and for those that I come in contact with.

As part of my mission, I founded The Chopra Center. My mission: to educate health professionals, patients and the general public on the connection between the relationship of mind, body, and spirit and healing. I teach people how to find their inner-self (most people have lost touch with theirs). When we find our inner-self, we find the wisdom that our bodies can be wonderful pharmacies – creating wonderful drugs – you name it, the human body can make it in the right does, at the right time, for the right organ without side effects.

The body is a network of communication. Our thoughts influence everything that happens in our body. The problem is many people automatically assume, "All I have to do is think positively, and everything will be fine." Because many assume this, they become unnatural and pretend everything is okay.

One must go beyond that; one must experience silence. It is when one experiences silence healing energies become involved and a balance is created. Psalms 46:10 says, "Be still and know that I am God". When the body is silent, it knows how to repair itself.

Pursuing my mission gives me fulfillment. It makes me whole. It makes me feel that I will continue to do what I have been doing. If I had all the time and money in the world, this is I what I would choose to do. It gives me joy and a connection to the creative bar of the universe. I have realized that the pursuit of my goals is the progressive expansion of happiness.

Pursue your goals and find your happiness, wholeness, and balance in this world.

Deepak Chopra, M.D.

My Journey to Self-Discovery
Dr. Erika Duffy

I remember praying to God as a child, asking Him to help me help others, feeling at the same time I had no right asking for help myself. As a child, I hated myself. I felt my feelings didn't matter. I was forced to suppress them and never addressed the trauma of years of sexual, emotional and physical abuse. "Don't ever tell anyone," I was told. "No one will believe you. You should be grateful for having a roof over your head and food on the table." I blamed myself and felt I must be a bad person. I hoped that by asking God to help others, He would somehow help me too.

I did as I was told and kept silent, holding in my emotions. Self-loathing and shame consumed me. I learned to live always fearing for my life, or for those I loved. As I discovered, later in life, emotional problems can manifest themselves as physical ones. My first ones developed as a teenager when I suffered from depression and anxiety attacks. I was hospitalized with colitis and was told a colonostomy was being considered.

Problems kept developing. I suffered a spinal injury and was temporarily crippled. I developed vertigo, blackouts, post-traumatic stress disorder and could not leave my house. I was dying, with no one to help me! Then, with the near death of my daughter, I thought it couldn't get any worse. And then I was told about my real father.

My twin brother and I found him—my dad, with two new sisters and my step mom. The man who raised me was an imposter. I couldn't possibly deny what a great gift that was, discovering my true dad. But it left me feeling as though I had been robbed of the life that I could, maybe even should, have lived. Questions still remain unanswered. I confused my desperate self-image for reality and made poor choices to escape the pain of living with what I thought was myself. These feelings became my identity.

I bottomed out, feeling hopeless. The doctors could not help me, only offering pills. Then I began to realize that I was re-living my suppressed emotions. The more I resisted these emotions, the more intense they became. So, instead of suppressing these feelings, I learned how to connect with and release them. I stopped trying to control how I felt and instead started working with it. I then started to improve and realized I could feel better and wanted to teach others that they could stop suffering too.

I moved across the country, my travels becoming a journey for personal growth and self-understanding. I started working with brilliant teachers and mentors. I learned how we have emotional, mental, physical and spiritual bodies that are interconnected. I attended schools and learned techniques and tools to release trauma and negative patterns that interfere with our lives. I studied the unconscious mind and its influence over our lives, and how the physical body heals and changes when releasing emotions. I learned and identified with my spirit, knowing its purpose is to be happy. I now have a successful practice utilizing the skills I developed over the years from my experiences and training, helping others overcome their past and discover their true life of happiness. I discover more of my real self every day. I have a wonderful family and a beautiful home.

We can stay haunted by our past or we can use it as a tool to discover ourselves, our purpose and to create a happier life. If you are unhappy, know you have the power to change and release the past. Wake up and really live your life.

Dr. Erika Duffy

Certain Success

Arnie Pechler III

"*D*on't follow in footsteps, don't wait for a lead, just pick your own path, and then succeed!" These words are part of a poem my father presented to me thirty years ago on the day I graduated from high school.

Based on my track record as a senior, my father was either exhibiting extreme optimism or he wrote the poem the night before I graduated.

Like many teens and young adults, I had already begun to stray far from the path to success. Alcohol was causing me problems and preventing me from living up to my potential. The next seven years of excessive drinking brought me to a point of surrender. I did not like what I was doing or who I had become. I had not only fallen off the wagon; I had fallen far from the path.

From this bottom, with the help of a power greater than myself and several unselfish mentors and teachers, I have built a firm foundation for my pathway to success and live a life beyond my wildest dreams. I want to assure anyone who reads this, however, that I have not "arrived." Please consider me a fellow traveler enjoying the journey on the path to success.

My mission in life is to make a meaningful difference in the lives of those with whom I come in contact, and allow them to make a meaningful difference in my life. I help people pick their own paths to certain success, and advise them of the sharp curves, potholes, steep cliffs and the bridges that may be out, based on my experience traveling a parallel path.

Nearly everyone has success-derailing characteristics that prohibit or prevent them from becoming all that they can be. When the alcohol problem was removed from my life, I chose to build a new foundation on four cornerstones: integrity, responsibility, goals and faith. I learned that in order to have anything of value, you must first be a person of value, and then do something of value which helps others.

To become a person of value, I decided that I must live a consistent life. I was introduced to the concept that everyone has three different personalities, three "me's" if you will. The "me" who I really am, the "me" I reveal to others, and the "me" I would like to be. To the extent those three "me's" are in harmony, I am happy. If they are not in harmony, I need to take the appropriate action to bring them into harmony and live a life of integrity.

By taking an inventory of both my strengths and weaknesses, I was able to identify the threats that could prevent me from becoming the person I wanted to be. I became honest with myself, my wife, my parents, employer and friends and then accepted the responsibility to take action and change.

I developed a simple formula which has serves me well, A + A = I M; Awareness plus Action Equals Improved Me. The inverse formula is also enlightening. A + N A = M M; Awareness plus No Action Equals Miserable Me.

In this process, I learned that money is a key ingredient in many goals and something I needed to learn more about. I took action and became a Certified Financial Planner and earned a Master's Degree in business administration. Applying this knowledge and sharing it with others has enabled me to achieve financial freedom and help many other people do the same. I expose people to real tools for the real word of money and time management.

I learned to practice the triple ten percent rule; ten percent of income to church or charity, ten percent to savings and ten percent for self-development. This discipline has given me the means to capitalize on many opportunities that have presented themselves over the years.

These wonderful events in my life have been made possible by both action and faith. Although faith is the last cornerstone in my foundation for success, I will not be presumptuous, or narrow minded, and describe or define faith. One thing I can share from my own experience is that what we look for in life is what we usually find. Please be careful what you are looking for and pick your own path in the area of faith.

Having been on the path to success for many years, I am grateful that I now live, at least most days, happy, joyous, and free.

I was reminded of this privilege one evening a few years ago when I pulled into the driveway of my house on the lake. My three-year-old granddaughter came running across the driveway with a big smile on her face. Myrrhia jumped into my arms, gave me a big kiss, and said, "Papa is a lucky boy." I said, "Why is Papa a lucky boy?" My granddaughter said, "Because Myrrhia loves him."

Indeed "Papa" is a lucky boy. Success and happines will be certain for you also if you pick your own path carefully and follow it faithfully. Enjoy the journey!

Arnie Pechler III, MBA, CFP, LUTCF, LLIF

Wake up... Live the Life You Love, Living on Purpose

A Life in Healing
Ann Taylor

As a child, if someone had asked me to imagine 10 possible careers I might one day enter, "energy healer" would have shown up somewhere between trapeze artist and Mezzo-Soprano, if it showed up at all.

Imagine my surprise when I first became aware of this gift after a dozen or so years working as a stockbroker. During that time, I had attained everything our culture tells us we should strive for: a fantastic apartment, a snazzy car, a wonderful guy, an extravagant income, not to mention every single gadget, appliance and plaything under the sun.

And yet a crucial piece of the puzzle was missing: a spiritual life, a connection with something loftier than the fast-pedaling, type-A lifestyle I was leading. Like many before me, my all-consuming interest in energy work sprang from a discontent with material conquest, and from the realization that tending properly to the soul – your own and other people's – is ultimately the only goal worth pursuing.

For years, I'd laughingly told people that my family of origin put the "D" in the word "dysfunctional." Having survived an abusive childhood and come out the other side of just about every emotional issue and block there is, wasn't I uniquely qualified to help other people achieve the lives they were meant to live?

At first I dug in my heels. The worldly life I was leading (but not loving) was enticing, and, in its own way, addicting. After a weekend of "training," which I really didn't want to attend, I came home and began working with people, doing hands on healing and instantaneously achieving results that astounded both my clients and me. It was the beginning of an all-consuming, profoundly gratifying career that has completely transformed my life along with countless others.

I've been an energy practitioner for almost a decade now, doing energy healing work with approximately 10,000 people. In the first year alone I traveled the country leading countless workshops, including one with Dr. Bernie Siegel, where, with the help of the Jesus Christ, I connected intimately to a crowd of nearly 1,000 people. These days, I work with people from my home office, treating a wide range of issues. One client asks me to heal a lifetime of depression and low self-esteem. Another wants me to heal her of the overwhelming feeling that nothing she ever does is good enough. A third, a freelance writer, requests my help in overcoming his fear of failure, his perennial anxiety that he'll never get another magazine assignment and fall hopelessly behind in his rent. A fourth comes on behalf of her husband, who's paralyzed by indecision. It is possible to heal people on the telephone, through the medium of those close to them. Most of the work I do, in fact, is on the phone. The unnumbered testimonials I receive attest to the power of the work I do, or rather, that Jesus Christ performs through me.

Today, I can honestly say I wouldn't surrender the gift of this wonderful life for anything in the world. Not only is the work intensely rewarding – I love my clients, I can create my own hours, and I earn a gratifyingly large income. But recently I've taken steps to expand my business by performing international tele-seminars where I'm able to heal countless people simultaneously. I never imagined entering this career, and now I use it to serve God in the best way possible.

Ann Taylor

Shoulda, Coulda, Woulda

Nancy Abercrombie

*I*n our house, guilt was served at breakfast. Mother doled it out in buckets. When she was 94, she finally admitted to me that nothing is solved by guilt. Even so, it was a huge surprise when she loved my song about guilt which I sent to all of my relatives.

Chorus:
Shoulda-Coulda-Woulda done this or that
That's too bad - Tit for tat
Shoulda-Coulda-Woulda just gone to bat
Shoulda-Coulda-Woulda done that

Some haven't talked to me since. No big deal. Nobody ever talked directly to anybody. When you wanted to communicate to Sister Number Five, you began talking to Sister Number Two, and so on until everything was a big mess and the truth went missing.

I thought everybody had a built-in guilt mechanism. Every other sentence I uttered used some form of those three little words, "shoulda-coulda-woulda. "I'm sorry," was carved into my forehead.

Shoulda-Coulda-Woulda done this or that
I forgot Oughta Not
Oughta Not, Shoulda Not, Coulda Not, Woulda Not
Done anything at all

When we are tiny people, "oughta not" is a good control to protect us when we might hurt ourselves. But it carries over into all the areas where goals and fun lives. Burdened by so many "oughta nots," we can wind up doing nothing at all.

Other people always know the way to run your life
So they fill your head with guilt, to just keep you in line
Carefully they feed you until you have learned enough
To manufacture guilt all by yourself.

How any of us survived is a mystery. Mother had PMS every day of her life. Her hormones were always raging, demonstrating themselves in anger, frustration, brow-beating or crying. Her need for love was not satisfied, I suppose, because she had to ask for a hug before bedtime. Poor mama. But, what a master at martyrdom!

Shoulda-Coulda-Woulda Chorus.....

When this song was born, Mother was the first one to hear it. I had to make a special recording for her and she played it for everyone.

So maybe I shoulda - But I really didn't want to
And maybe I coulda - If things went differently
And maybe I woulda - But I wasn't motivated
That doesn't change the way I think of me
That doesn't make me stupid and it doesn't make me lazy
It doesn't change the way I think of me

What a relief and what a great revelation. Its OK if I do not fulfill whatever someone else expects of me. I think we are conditioned to fill our guilt box. I never got away with, "I don't want to." While living under "my parent's roof," free will was not an option. Oh, the joys of being a dysfunctional family!

Oh, Shoulda-Coulda-Woulda is a waste of time
A waste of yours, a waste of mine
Shoulda-Coulda-Woulda is just old hat
And who needs more of that? !

Here, here! The world has learned all it needs to know through manipulation. I have one word for guilt-makers: Patooey! Get a life!

There is so much we can do that is productive, fulfilling, and brings joy to others. I've decided to forgive myself for whatever I might have done, or not done. I have eons to fulfill my spiritual self, to achieve my soul's purpose. I will try being nice to myself. Sounds like fun.

Nancy Abercrombie

The Grandmaster's Secrets

Ron Smith

I have never, until today, shared these truths with anyone but my wife and children, however now it's time.

I'm blessed to live a wonderful, exciting, adventure filled life. I have an exceptional wife and large loving family. I live in a community where the median home value is right around 1 million dollars. My children have tutors and take tennis lessons from the greatest, most successful coach in the world. I'm a real estate investor; I own successful businesses and am beginning new ventures all the time. We are living our dreams. But life was not always so good.

I spent the years up through college living in poverty, moving yearly from one rented apartment to another. We always had old used cars that sometimes got repossessed. I never made close friends because I didn't want anyone to know where I lived. I lived with constant shame, self-doubt, low self-esteem and fear. But my life changed forever and so can yours...if you'll follow the lessons I was fortunate enough to learn from a very special man.

It is said, "...when the pupil is ready, the master will appear." I met him in my early 30s as I was making advances in the work force but was destined to live an ordinary existence. I earned a good salary but was living paycheck to paycheck and had the nagging feeling that life was passing me by. Many of you can probably relate to these feelings. Then I met a very spiritual and amazing man who I thought was only going to teach me martial arts. Since he is now advanced in age and values his privacy, I will introduce him simply as: the Grandmaster.

The Grandmaster was an expert in an exotic and deadly Southeast Asian martial art. Watching him perform was like looking at poetry personified. He was powerful, fluid, graceful and frighteningly proficient. He was also disarmingly charming, gracious, funny, patient and kind. Weekly instruction under the Grandmaster was grueling, demanding, painful and satisfying. Over time, however, I discovered the Grandmaster was adept at much more than martial arts; he also owned quite a few businesses, was an expert at marketing, owned hundreds of investment real estate units, and was expert in mental programming and self-esteem. He was a self-made multi-millionaire and eventually became my mentor in not only the martial arts but the financial arts as well.

Over the past 10 or so years, the Grandmaster has taught me many life altering lessons. A few of the Grandmaster's Secrets to improve your life physically, spiritually, financially, mentally, and relationally are:

Secret #1   *Masters Live by the Trinity Triangle*

All areas of life must be balanced and developed equally and simultaneously: spiritual, physical and mental. Feed and nourish all three constantly. This secret applies to the martial as well as financial arts. You will have an abundant life if you apply this principal.

Secret #2   *Masters Must Learn to Fight Imaginary Opponents*

Developing your skill in visualization and imagery is the key to mastery in any endeavor. The Grandmaster spent hours fighting against invisible or imaginary opponents and taught me to do the same. He also taught me to imagine daily—in the most vivid, precise detail—the future I wished for myself and my family. Visualization is essential in fighting the opponents of poverty and lack.

Secret #3   *Masters Focus on the Fundamentals*

It's not the big things that create breakthroughs, it's the little things perfected and performed extraordinarily well. In all of the key areas of your life, focus on the most basic components and master them. Eat the elephant one bite at a time.

These are only a few of the Grandmaster's secrets. He taught me dozens of them. The important thing to know is this: no matter where you are in your life, you can make a decision—this instant—to begin to apply the Grandmaster's secrets and live beyond your wildest dreams.

I wish you powerful, profitable and prosperous living.

Ron Smith (Guro)

Wake Up

John Picard

Wake-up - The alarm has gone off. 6:00 a.m. is flashing like a detour sign pointing away from your dreams. Where did the dreams go? When did motivation become survival? How can I regain that passion of purpose and mission?

Making your life whole again - You don't have to choose between work and life. You can bring them together and weave the vitality of your business into all of the rest of the tapestry of your life. Success and reaching the next stage does not mean losing sight of what's important. This opportunity comes from focusing on the power of your relationships.

Business is personal - The movies tell you: "It's only business, it's nothing personal." Despite every advancement in technology, nothing has ever beaten the human connection. Business is personal. Your ability to manifest and grow relationships around your dreams is everything.

Reaching up from deep inside - Each of us walks a path toward purpose and success. Driven by a life crisis or mentor, there comes a moment on that path, a tipping point, where you know its right. Nothing stops you when you are in these moments. The flow and creativity is almost addicting.

Being true - My own path began late at night as a boy. My father was a strong character, one who laughed well and demanded that the product of my efforts be true to my self and my capabilities.

The ring of truth - Often, the night before a school assignment was due, we would sit in the living room together as I faced the third draft, and a few hysterics. He would encourage me to go beyond the expectations of a teacher and find an answer that had a 'ring of truth' about it. We wouldn't stop until there was a synergy and a flow to the answers that seemed to miraculously come from my lips. We all have had moments like these, when the words come of themselves, when you ran faster than ever before. Is there anything closer to purpose than these moments?

Huh? - However, when I was 12, it sometimes just reached the point where I couldn't hear my father anymore. Noticing my eyes glazing, he would stand in front of me with a glint in his eyes and a barely controlled smile, and yell back, "Listen louder... listen louder."

Listening every day - That stopped me. After a moment and a forced smile, I got it. Real listening is action, not just waiting your turn. To this day, I see every relationship as an opportunity to listen to the meaning that lies beneath and between words.

Touchpoints - I have turned these skills into a marketing career devoted to client success. As a 'relationship architect,' I help clients 'listen louder' and manage all the customer touchpoints. Every company's greatest asset is the sum of their relationships. From marketing to service, it is amazing the power when you align yourself around your relationships. From the latest technology to a simple handshake, it all grows from the human side of the business equation.

Weave it all together - More than revenues or growth, my most profound success often comes from my personal investment in the human connections. I recently received a call from an executive who had been a client-partner for several years. He couldn't reach his wife and needed to be driven home from a hospital emergency. As we drove back together that day, I knew I had heard his message of trust and that I was living my own teachings. I had woven the meaning of my life into my business.

Can you hear it - You have your own path to walk. Listen for the messages of your relationships. They are the sound of your alarm going off. It is time to get out of bed. Time to wake up and dream!

John L. Picard

Living from the Heart
Dr. Judith Moore

I am a radiant, powerful, passionate, inspiring woman of light. I know this, and this is what I live by. But I didn't always know it.

I grew up trying to be a good girl. I wanted to obey all the "shoulds." I developed a very strong sense of what I should do and what I shouldn't, how I should look and how I shouldn't, how I should act and how I shouldn't, the type of people I should be with and the type I shouldn't. I wanted to please my parents, family, friends, and God. Because of this, I carried a strong sense of guilt. I dwelt on all the things I had done that I shouldn't, and all the things I didn't do that I should. I was "shoulding" all over myself, and the effect was a strong dislike of myself and a sense of failure.

As a mother of six young children, I was drowning in an overwhelming ocean. No matter how much I cleaned, the house was dirty. As often as I taught my children to behave, they would misbehave. As soon as I committed to stop yelling at my family, I would explode again. I would go on a diet, then binge and put the weight all back on. I couldn't do anything right. I felt unloved and unappreciated. I became very depressed because of all my "weaknesses," and my family reacted to my pain. My husband considered leaving me. A young son was caught shoplifting. A sweet daughter had severe outbursts of rage that frightened me. My other children seemed out of control.

Near the breaking point, I asked a friend to watch my younger children while the older ones were in school. I spent the day in my bedroom, crying and pleading with God to lift the burdens that engulfed me. My pain allowed me to open my heart and listen. Slowly, through my tears, God began to teach me.

Through my heart, God taught me something that I had never before considered. He taught me that He gave me my weaknesses, and they had a purpose. He taught me that because He gave me weaknesses to experience in mortal life, He wasn't disappointed in me because of them. What my weaknesses were teaching me was His kind of love, love without condition or expectation. He taught me that I was to first begin loving myself by being grateful for my weaknesses, for they were serving me as much as my strengths were. I was to let go of all the "shoulds" that my weaknesses kept me from doing, and live by listening to and trusting the gentle promptings of my heart.

My feelings began to shift as I asked my heart what activity would serve the highest good, rather than trying to do everything my ego mind told me I "should" do. I began to focus on my strengths rather than my weaknesses. By following the promptings of my heart, I learned over time how to renew my relationship with my husband, and love him because of his weaknesses as well as his strengths. I learned to let go of needing my children to be perfect. My purpose as their mother was simply to love them, teach them, be an example for them, and learn from them.

Soon after, by following the promptings of my heart, I found myself in medical school. By following my heart, I also learned alternative forms of medicine. I experienced the joy of seeing people heal as they took responsibility for their health and their lives by following the promptings of their own hearts. I am now in the process of creating a medical school that integrates both western and alternative medicine, a school that teaches students to follow their hearts and to heal with love.

But more than all of this, by living from my heart I am living in peace, joy, and gratitude. Rather than accomplishing all the things I "should" do, I have learned how to simply Be. I am finally in love with myself.

Judith S. Moore, D.O.

Finding Balance in Life

Tom Tessereau

Science is the study of life. All the sciences point to life as predictable, relying on immutable principles or laws. As you mature and grow mentally and spiritually you realize that there are rules or principles by which life can be lived for maximum experience. There are principles for loving relationships, good health, wealth and happiness too. Understanding these simple principles can put an end to the suffering and struggling that you see so often in your world, in your culture, and in your life. It can aid your journey to realizing your true purpose.

One of the simplest rules is that life is a whole living organism and that anything that affects any part affects the whole. If one child is favored at the expense of the other children the whole family suffers. In business, if one department is ignored the entire organization declines. Your life is to be lived in balance! In Western culture, the pursuit of material or monetary gains at the expense and neglect of the health, emotional well-being and spiritual connection is a great source of suffering. Later in life comes the realization that money and material goods did not bring lasting happiness, loving relationships or good health.

Similarly, it is unbalanced to only pursue spiritual practices and ignore the needs of your business and family. Likewise, it is limiting to retreat to intellectual knowledge and to believe that understanding or the ability to analyze is living fully. This is a classic example of the disconnection of mind and body. There is no joy in understanding. True joy is living life fully and in balance.

Bringing awareness to what is missing in your life balance can be as simple as quietly asking, "If I were lacking in one dimension, which would it be: physical, mental, emotional, or spiritual?" Now that you know where you are deficient, ask, "What can I do to develop that part of myself?" Then trust the answer. Make a commitment to create more balance. Do not be afraid to ask for assistance or guidance. If you don't allow others to assist, you deny them the joy and satisfaction you receive when you assist others. In essence you are actually helping others when you let them help.

Another universal principle often misunderstood is "as you give you receive." The karmic cycle is more exact than you imagine, and is like planting seeds. "As you sow you reap," can be translated as, "What you sow you reap." Sometimes this is misinterpreted by thinking, "Why doesn't my spouse love and respect me? After all, I work long hours every day, and bring home the money." Providing materially sows a different crop than loving, accepting and nurturing emotionally. You cannot plant apple seeds and expect a cherry tree. Take a look at what you have been giving or sowing and what you are receiving in return. Or, look at what is missing in your world and investigate what you have been giving to others. If you want more love in your life, be more loving. If you want more financially, share, tithe and give generously. Helping others to be more prosperous brings more abundance. To be accepted, be more accepting. This approach to life allows you to see that you are ultimately responsible for your life and experiences and in this knowing is true empowerment!

Seek balance in every step on your life journey, breathe fully, smile often, love deeply, and keep planting the seeds for your magnificent harvest!

Tom Tessereau

AccidentalBusiness.com

Rebecca Fine

*I*n the spring of 1998, a man I'd never met sent me a little book that I'd never heard of. Published in 1910, it was written by a man who has been dead for almost ninety years.

That little book changed my entire life. As I began to put into practice the universal, spiritual principles of prosperity explained in that book, the results were astonishing, beginning quickly and continuing to this day.

But it wasn't just my own prosperity that snowballed. What happened next sparked a chain reaction that has spread to tens of thousands of people in 145 countries so far!

Before reading the book, I was mired in a thoroughly unoriginal state of mind known as the dreaded "midlife crisis." Feeling trapped in a business that was merely adequate, in terms of both income and satisfaction, I felt that there has to be more. My life must have more purpose than this. This mental sludge had me looking all over for answers. I hated the "stuck" sensation, the mundane and predictable nature of it.

Then the little book arrived—with answers.

After about a year or so of exploring and working with the principles I'd first learned about in *The Science of Getting Rich*, and enjoying the very tangible results, I felt they were sufficiently verified to share with others. I was so thrilled and excited with what had happened to me, I wanted everyone to have this little book.

So I invited readers of an e-zine that I'd been publishing for a couple of years to read the book and participate in an online discussion. These people were all in the same business I was in at the time and were well aware of the overnight success I had experienced, with my partner, in the recent past. Nearly 750 of them took me up on the invitation, and so began The Summer Science Project.

There was only one hitch. Everyone needed to read the book, and try as I might, I couldn't find a publisher willing to give 750 buyers a break on the price. So I tracked down the original 1910 edition, turned it into an e-book, and sent it to everyone by email.

I had no idea what I was getting myself into!

Strange, unexpected things started to happen. People were telling me, "I love this book, but I don't have time to read it every day. I wish I could just listen to it." Finally, in one of those blinding flashes of the obvious, I went into a recording studio. This was beginning to get serious. As more and more people around the world read, or heard, the book, they began to ask questions. After about a year, I put together a tele-class series. A few hundred people quickly agreed to join.

But I soon realized that when you're trying to serve people all around the world, tele-classes are limiting. It's impossible to find a good time for everyone. Since I'd already seen the power of the Internet, I decided to turn my successful class into an online, international, multi-media, interactive course. But how to price it so anyone in any country and economy could participate?

The answer came in my morning meditation. I picked up my reading for that morning: the 1932 book *Prosperity* by Charles Fillmore. His opinion was that any work of a spiritual nature should have a price; that there should be a fair exchange. But if there were no substantial fixed costs, then payment should be on what he called "a love offering" basis.

Bingo! Would-be students will get their first lesson before they're even enrolled. They'll have to seriously consider and determine their own proper tuition!

So that's how it's gone, these last two years. Thousands of people from all over the world have paid anywhere from $2 to $1,000 and all sums in between. And I've had the immense joy of getting to know people from all over the world, from almost every kind of background imaginable, watching as they begin to shift their thinking, find joy and transform their lives for the better.

What began as a simple desire to share something wonderful with as many as possible has turned into an unexpected, thoroughly satisfying, very profitable, "accidental business" that has now expanded into a network of related Web sites serving people in, at last count, 145 countries.

Better yet, without any sudden moment of epiphany, but just in quiet, peaceful, joyful realization, I came to know that my life's purpose had found me. By following my inner guidance and using my God-given talents in new ways, I've magically awakened to find myself spending my days doing what I love. Now I am creating new projects on my own and with others, building new Web sites, publishing more books filled with forgotten wisdom and writing articles, and getting to "talk" with more than 100,000 people around the world about how the spiritual and the material are merely different aspects of the same amazing Power that creates, sustains, animates and regulates the entire universe.

Rebecca Fine
copyright 2004

From Rags to Riches

Vrisayda Porshu Boggess, Ph.D.c

*F*rom eating beans to eating at the Ritz Carlton; from wearing hand-me-downs to shopping at exclusive department stores, who would have known where life's journey was to take me? Hypnosis is now my path; empowering people is my destiny. Loving what I do is who I am, and I am what I do.

Find the true meaning and purpose in whatever you do. Meaning will come into your life when you love who you are and what you are doing. View problems as opportunities for growth by paying attention to what you learn from past situations. I have learned to welcome challenges that demonstrate what I need to change in myself to make me a better person. Over the years, I have trusted a higher power to lead me, not always knowing, or liking, where I was going.

I was born into a family considered quite poor by today's standards. Life was a little tough for us. Father worked at a steel mill and my mother, after learning some English, got a job working in an elementary school cafeteria. That was nice because sometimes she could bring home some of the leftover food for us. Hand-me-downs and homemade clothes made up my wardrobe. My parents taught us good values, morals, ethics and compassion; plus we were strong in love and faith—definitely the cornerstone of a good beginning.

When I needed to find a job, I wanted it to be something in which I could help people in some way. Working as a dental assistant, I began my journey of helping people. That, however, seemed empty, so I did some part-time modeling, and I loved the make-up and dressing up.

In 1977, the modeling led to cosmetology school where I became one of the first licensed estheticians in California. I was fortunate to do what I liked and was making money at it when no one knew what an esthetician, or facials, were. I ran my own business from the day I received my esthetician. When I opened my clinic, About Face Skin Care, it was the only facial clinic in all of Orange County, and the Yellow Pages listings did not even have a category for my type of business. Everyone in the shopping center where I had my business thought I was going to fail and be the first one out of business. Failure was not the picture I had. My mind-set was belief in what I was doing and the expectancy of success. What you believe in and expect, you can achieve.

I had some other keys to success. I already knew how to work hard, and people knew I was honest, so my business succeeded greatly. I really loved working with my clients. People rave about the custom treatments and products that I've been providing for them for nearly three decades.

During the course of my work, I became a Reiki Master, providing healing energy treatments. My clients felt that the face and shoulder massage they received during their facials was the most restful time in their whole month. Clients said they could tell that I really loved what I was doing. Everything seemed great. I was making lots of money by doing what I loved and just being me. God and the Universe just seemed to bless me. The Universe provides but still you must have awareness and take action. As much as I love doing facials, I knew that I had to do more for my clients. During the years, I would hear stories of how stressful life was with its many issues. I wanted to help on a deeper level, to really make a difference. So my life, my journey, evolved.

One day I received an invitation to a workshop on being certified as a spiritual counselor held by Dr. Doreen Virtue at the American Institute of Hypnotherapy in Irvine, California. At the institute, I noticed the literature on becoming a hypnotherapist and immediately knew this was what I was destined to do. Thirty years prior, I read books on hypnosis, and went to a hypnotherapist myself. A strong power was pulling me in the direction of hypnosis. I can't explain it but knew it was something that I needed to do. When you know something you need to do, and you want it deep down in your heart, the Universe will support you. Here is where faith comes in, not only in a higher power, but also in yourself. Know that synchronicity in your life has a purpose.

I have worked in the hypnotherapy field now for seven years. I am a Ph.D. candidate in clinical hypnotherapy and have helped many people help themselves by changing their lives through the power of their minds. I never dreamed that I would become a doctor of clinical and medical hynotherapy. Or, in the back of my mind, did I know it all along?

God, the Universe, and the power of my unconscious mind have guided me all along. There is purpose in my life, and in your life too. Look within, and you will find it; purpose already exists.

Vrisayda Porshu Boggess, Ph.D.c

Out of tragedy, purpose

Dr. Robert Powell

My story began two years ago when my partner, Caroline, was diagnosed with cancer. In that instant our lives turned around, not just upside down, but back to front and inside-out as well. With one finger permanently on the fast forward button, life would never be the same again.

The ordeal for Caroline, both physically and mentally, was immense. She underwent three operations to remove the cancer, nearly dying from an MRSA septicemia following one of the operations. Six bouts of chemotherapy and seven weeks of radiotherapy concluded with 24hrs of internal beam "annihilation." As a young couple, you just don't expect to face such trials and tribulations.

During all of this, I was, ironically, in the middle of my training to be a general practitioner, doing a six month rotation in Obstetrics and Gynecology at the local community hospital. I was seeing women bringing life into the world, and, at the same time, seeing life taken away from women with the same condition as Caroline. Somehow, I had to make sense of it all. The most caring and loving person I had ever met was fighting for her life and, even as a doctor, I felt powerless to help.

You see, there's something about cancer, or any serious illness/event, that forces you to re-examine your purpose in life and start asking yourself the really important questions, like, "Why am I here?" and "What's it all about?" When you do this you will almost always focus more on values such as love, health and happiness above any materialistic considerations.

I resorted to what I knew best, the scientific approach, which involved reading every medical book or journal on the subject. Trawling through every conceivably relevant web site on the net for what seemed like an eternity. I was looking for any ray of hope or morsel of information that would improve her chances of survival. It was around this time I also started to read books and listen to CD's on personal development and discovered the work of Deepak Chopra and Bill Harris, which helped me enormously to make sense of what was happening in my life.

I know that we've all read in other personal development books that it is the actions we take, as a result of the decisions we make, that score us the goals in life. And, of course, this is often easier said than done. However, unless you get this belief deeply embedded into that "muscle" they call your brain, changes and "living the dream" will never be easy. It is the ability to take action and discover your own life's purpose that will make a difference in the quality of your life.

I am very pleased to write that Caroline has made a full recovery, and is now healthier and more beautiful than she has ever been. She recently took over the running of a new business with great success. And as a result of our experiences together and the inspiration I gained from Caroline's courage, I am now fulfilling my own purpose in life, having set up a brand new health service in the United Kingdom called the "people's health service" (www.thephs.com) to be launched in September 2004. The mission/vision is to help make a difference in people's health by empowering them to take better care of their own mind body and soul, and generate much needed revenue to sow back into health facilities in local communities. In fact, you might even call it the "Robin Hood" health service.

Dealing with the uncertainties associated with cancer, or any life-threatening illness/event, can be mentally crippling unless you take action. One of the keys to success in the whole healing process is to take an active role in the rebalancing of the mind, body and soul, and to do whatever it takes to regain your health. This is not something that simply happens by passive osmosis, you've actually got to get out there and make it happen. Find out about the illness, learn about your mind and focus on those things that make you healthy and happy.

Dr. Robert S Powell

Everything You Want is on the Other Side of Fear!

Alice Wheaton, MA

*I*t was a warm August night, and I was on my way to work in the emergency room. I had been a nurse for six years and that day, as on so many days recently, I felt a call to a different life. All of my musings were set aside when an ambulance arrived with several victims of a traffic accident. The lovely woman I was attending to, who was not seriously injured, had been on her way to a party at a yacht club. I was impressed by her elegant and prosperous style so I asked her what she did for a living. She told me she was in sales with Bell Yellow Pages. Sales, a notion that somehow felt right even though I had never considered it as a vocation before. I wondered aloud, "Do you think I could do that?"

With a few words she changed my life forever: "You can obviously handle stress and challenging situations so you could be good in sales. Why don't you go to Xerox and give them my husband's name. He's a sales manager there; they'll interview you out of respect for him, but they won't hire you because you are a woman, and they are not hiring women in sales yet. Nevertheless, the interview process would be good for you when looking for sales jobs at other companies, including where I work."

The next day I went to Xerox Canada in Toronto and applied for a job. After nine interviews, and dogged determination on my part, I finally won the position – the first woman on my team and in that branch of Xerox Canada. Thus began my career and my love affair with the game of sales. From my start as an award-winning sales representative, nearly thirty years ago, I have progressed to the satisfaction of being the president of my own sales training and consulting company.

From the first day at Xerox, I realized that I was way out of my league. My previous education and work experience did not prepare me for a life in the sales bullpen. I went from working with all women to working with all men, and I definitely felt I had much to prove. Since fear, doubt and insecurity were my constant companions, I decided to embrace them and take the action I needed to be successful, despite their presence. Before long, I had developed processes and systems that helped transform my fear into courage, passion and action.

I discovered that defying fear gave me courage which was a fertile ground on which my passion could flourish. Without passion, I would not have been able to tap into the inspiration and the willingness to move out of my comfort zone and develop new skills; I would not have been able to take action and pay the price that would lead to long-term success. For the past fifteen years I have had the mission, and honour, of teaching other people how to do the same.

What one thing could you do if fear, doubt and insecurity no longer stopped you?

My experience with thousands of salespeople and other top performers has proven to me that transforming fear of rejection, fear of failure and fear of self-promotion is critical to their success. All of our dreams require risk, which usually involves fear. I have observed that the reward for transforming fear into courage is the increased ability to move forward with ease and grace.

Thirty years after my discussion with the patient in the emergency room, I was ready to publish my second book called, *Say NO to Me! The True Power of UpSide-Down Selling!* I wanted to acknowledge the woman who had changed my life so profoundly. I remembered her name and that she was going to a party at a yacht club so I phoned yacht clubs throughout Ontario, and finally found the club where she was still a member.

When I called to express my gratitude, she did not remember me. We discussed how simple kindnesses and words of encouragement can have a ripple effect that reaches far beyond sight or imagination. That brief encounter truly affirmed to me that everything we want is on the other side of fear! What would you do today if you had more courage? And if not now, when?

Alice Wheaton

A Moment of Transition

Jerrold H. Nowacki

*O*ne thing I know for sure is that life's transitions do not always make sense. But the many threads of experiences are woven into the personal fabric of our lives. There are enigmatic forces of a divine nature at work living within the heart of every human being. As we strengthen our faith, mental and emotional energies, the quality of our beliefs expand into a creation, forming our spiritual purpose and aligning our life's destiny.

I awoke one morning with a strange unsettled feeling. Not a physical ache, but an emotional strain. A foreboding feeling swept through me like a dry coarse wind. I couldn't help but think something unexpected was about to happen. I shook off my feelings of uneasiness and uncertainty and began visualizing positive images unfolding into the events shaping my day.

The day at work went along normally as I drove from the resort where I held a position in timeshare sales; however, I couldn't get my mind off of my friend Howard. Howard was a great inspiration, not only to me, but to everyone on the sales team at our resort.

Howard was recently reassigned to our Lake Arrowhead California property to help manage sales. He was the guy who everyone knew, including you, because he created the Smiley face button. This guy was dynamic; sort of a legend and a real giver.

As I opened my door upon returning to the apartment, the phone rang and that uneasy feeling suddenly reappeared and shot through me with an added sense of sadness. A friend from the resort called to inform me that Howard had suffered a heart attack and was rushed to the hospital in Los Angeles. Two days later he died of complications from the attack.

I was in shock and disbelief, but, at the same time, I could feel Howard's presence. I heard his voice inside me loud and clear, "Jerry, remember this position is temporary. After all you're a leader. You have the power within to move mountains and to create. Soon you will realize that power. And you will use that power to, once again, empower others.

I couldn't get his words out of my head? What did he mean? Several days after Howard passed away the resort manager called me into his office and asked if I would like to replace Howard. I immediately thought, "Howard can't be replaced." That guy was Mr. Charisma to the "max." Yes, my background is in sales training, sales management and public speaking, but replace Howard? I was so caught off guard I told the resort manager I needed to have a day to think about his proposal. As I walked out the door he said, "You are under-utilized here, and it's a great opportunity for you to succeed in your own domain, doing what you do best. And Jerry, Howard would have wanted you to be the one to replace him." You see, I was struggling personally with many emotional issues that made me question every aspect of my being. Even though I had my own past success in business with my seminar and training company, my faith was shaky. Now, on top of it all, I was hearing voices.

That evening as I rested, contemplating my options, a very strong presence came into my room and, as I sat there in almost a trance like state, a gentle voice came to me and said, "Yes Jerry, I'm the one who carries you when you think that you can't make it."

I slept soundly. Confidently, the next morning, I accepted the position and immediately headed for our Lake Arrowhead resort. It was like magic. Everything fell into place with my role as trainer, coach and sales manager. From day one I began hiring and training people, preparing them for great sales and income opportunities. I am pleased to say that this once-struggling resort and myself were both once again abundant.

In moments of transition I now turn to the poem *Footprints in the Sand*, I know, with confidence, who carries me when I can't make it.

Jerrold H. Nowacki

Change your Mind
Jennifer King

After a light aircraft crash, from which my husband, two grandchildren and I had a very lucky escape, I was repeatedly asked "why" are you not stressed and traumatized? We even made an appearance on the national news as the "feel good story."

My grandson Luke expressed his feelings as, "Awesome! That was the best ride I have ever had!" Colin, my husband, flew again five days later, I had to wait longer because of two compression fractures in my back and extensive bruising. Rebekah my granddaughter still likes to go flying.

I am an "ordinary person," having experienced most of the dramas and fear of life as a single parent to six children.

About ten years ago my health began to deteriorate. I become so ill I could not function, at all. After consulting many doctors, having the various recommended tests, procedures, operations and volumes of drugs, I was advised that nothing more could be done.

So I was more ill than I had ever been.

I began a search for information within the complementary health sector, the understanding of which has profoundly changed my life.

The right information just flowed into my life. I read endlessly and began training as a psychotherapist. Finally, I was able to assess what the real problems with my health were.

The training I have completed has enabled me to change the health and life-direction of family members and friends, also to begin working as a psychoanalyst, health educator and public speaker; work that I really enjoy.

I feel as though every event of my sometimes-turbulent life has been for a reason. Without realizing it, my life has been on purpose all the time. All my life experiences have a meaning now.

It is my quest to pass this information on to others. I have designed a program and book that illustrates how to implement this uncomplicated process which can change the entire life-direction of anyone.

Change is not just about dealing with 'bad' events and memories, but about thought design, management and projection.

It is important to not only explain how to change your mind, but also why the process functions the way it does. I offer an unprecedented, and direct, explanation of how we all have the inherent ability to choose and direct our success, health and well being. It is a comparison across time and cultures that unlocks the knowledge of how we function and grow, a simple plan to connect with yourself and to achieve health, wealth and happiness.

To the amazement of my health professionals, I have managed my recovery from the airplane crash without painkillers, using the Holosync Solution CD's meditation program and just the sheer pleasure of being me.

This could not be more different from the person I was just a little while ago, ill, living on medication and totally confused and disorientated about my life and life purpose.

Now my vision is to see everyone has the opportunity to *Wake Up... Live the Life You Love.*

You deserve it!

Jennifer King

Making a Difference
Stacey Roberts

*I*t was a beautiful Midwestern summer afternoon as I walked with my best friend. We were both 14 at the time. It was a normal day, just like any other. My friend and I laughed hysterically and talked endlessly. What I didn't know at the time was how I would often reflect on this moment throughout my life. It was the first time I had a glimpse of what my purpose here on this planet was meant to be. And it was the first step to living the life that I love today.

As we walked, we talked about the distant future—which was an unusual topic for adolescents. Normally the future, for us, was limited to the few months ahead. We chatted about what we might be doing: professions such as school teacher, doctor or nurse. Suddenly, I stopped in mid-sentence saying, "I know I am meant to make a difference in people's lives. Whatever I do, I know I will be helping people." Now, I am the first to admit that this isn't earth-shattering stuff, but it has guided me throughout my life and has been a determining factor in choosing the paths that I have taken.

And though I may have caught a small glimpse of my purpose at a relatively early age, it turned out to be a double edged sword until I got the rest of the message that led to the fulfilment I now experience each day.

So how could this be a double edged sword? If making a difference in people's lives was truly my purpose, wasn't fulfilling this purpose supposed to make me feel good inside? Why did I secretly hate myself in high school even though I tried to help anyone who needed it? Or, later in life, why at the end of the day did I continually feel something was missing even though I truly enjoyed working with the athletes that I coached and the patients that I treated as a physical therapist? If I was living my purpose, then why did I get so burned out? And why was I over $40,000 in credit card debt and in a financial mess? The money is just supposed to flow in when you are living your purpose, right? Ah, not exactly.

Almost 20 years later, I got the rest of the message. It didn't appear as overtly as the first message because, as we grow older, we tend to let more conscious noise overpower the sound of our own voices. For many years I was so concentrating on helping others, that I was not helping myself. What was missing was me taking care of me while I took care of others. Once I realized it was okay to grow myself while helping others, it was as if I plugged a hole in my soul and began to live the life that I love.

Taking care of me involved discovering and realigning my values, changing my focus and eliminating all the old beliefs and negative emotions I created in my past which were holding me back. I don't have to sacrifice my own happiness and health for the benefit of others, but I can help others fulfil their potential while fulfilling my own. I now have a lot more to offer my family; my clients get the results they want and I am financially in a better position than ever. My life is truly blessed. I am living my purpose and have created a life that I love.

Stacey Roberts

My Three Wives

David Resnick

*T*he single most important aspect to every success in my life was making a decision. Even though it seemed easy it was the hardest part. Sometimes I did not feel that I deserved what I wanted or was afraid I would fail or could not quite imagine that it was possible. But every time I made a decision it happened.

As a very young boy I made my most important decision - that being spiritual, loving and living by the Golden Rule and the will of my heart would always be most important. I absolutely believe in these values and completely trust my heart to guide everything I do. These values have touched every part of my life and helped me not only to be successful at my business but also to overcome personal demons like addictions, anxiety, being overweight, etc. While I am extremely proud of these personal successes, they are not what make me most successful, these are not the things I dream about in bed at night, give me peace or make me a better human being and spirit. That comes from my three wives.

This may seem strange at first but let me explain. The most important decisions we make can be influenced by what society, religion or what other people tell us our values should be, and/or our emotions. While I appreciate and respect other values, I want to make important choices in my life with values I carefully choose for myself—not chosen by others. Emotions serve many critical needs, including a richer and deeper experience of life, but I do not want my emotions to control the important decisions in my life. Three marriages can really test one's convictions, but I was unwilling to throw away the valuable relationships I had developed with my ex-wives because the marriage did not work, and I refused to consider these as "failed" marriages or look at myself, or ex-wives, as failures. We had too much invested to lose more than the marriage. We had children, we had history, and we still cared about each other!

Don't get me wrong I would have felt equally proud of one successful marriage as I do having three, but the point is that I decided not to use society's or anyone else's perspective on what marriage should or should not be like. And because of this, I have a wonderful wife and two wonderful ex-wives. My ex-wives and I remain close both as parents and as friends. There was never any part in me that felt I needed to stop loving, respecting or enjoying my ex-wives just because our marriage did not work out. After all, we would not have married if we had not loved each other. And I did not allow the "rules" of society to dictate the relationships between my ex-wives or my current wife, which allows them to have great relationships.

I don't sweep under the rug the personal characteristics that make me a three time wedding planner; these are parts of myself that I use to become more aware about being human and compassionate. Which is a much more productive way of using my experiences than being an outcast, no good, or judging myself as unworthy. The point is that I have constructed my own mirror to look into and not allowed the mirrors of the society, religion or community I grew up in to dictate my personal worth. Consequently, I continue to have rewarding, loving relationships with everyone I have been close to in my life, including, and especially, myself.

David Resnick

Humanity's Team

Conrad Cain

*I*t is clearly apparent to me until about nine months ago, I had been hiding from others, and from myself, waiting for a comfortable and safe situation where I could be myself and do what is so deeply ingrained in my heart, mind and spirit. I had been paralyzed by fear and was waiting for others to do what I felt that I could not. I had been waiting for the day that someone would create a space where I would be able step up to the plate and actually do something, not just be something, in my heart and mind that I was hiding from others and myself.

After reading *Communion with God* and hearing Neale speak on his book tour, *New Revelations* in Atlanta, I found myself called to Oregon for the first Humanity's Event in 2003. I can still clearly remember how I was profoundly touched at that event not only from the great love and energy that surrounded it, but also from the following words on posters around the complex, "Never doubt that a small group of dedicated citizens can change the world, and that, indeed, it's the only thing that ever has," (Margaret Mead) along with, "If not me who? If not now, when? Even though I had read these words before they took on a new and intensely clear meaning to me. An upwelling of Spirit filled my eyes with tears and my heart with the inspiration that now was the time for me to step forward, an inspired realization that, we were the ones I had been waiting for.

When I came back to Atlanta and started to travel and to talk to others about my experience in Oregon, I found that I was unable to articulate the reason for the new energy and conviction that I had brought back with me. It seemed that I was the only one (besides those others of us that had been there) that understood the passion of my intention. My confidence began to wane; I stepped back to see what might happen next. Christian Pankhurst showed up in my life late last year. Christian's passion was like a wind fanning the embers of my smoldering spiritual fire, and I became emblazoned with the intention to reinvent myself and to do anything and everything that I could to further this movement. It has been my intention, to stop just studying, being, and thinking about doing and start to do! Christian explained, "The doing is easy; it is the thinking about it that is hard." I realized from my past experiences that this was indeed true.

I have given up my past way of life in order to be of service to this cause, as Christian and many others have also done. I have learned just how powerful the power of intention can be and that whatever you can truly believe in, that you can achieve. I know that when one's intentions are in alignment with one's life mission, miracles will be manifested daily. I know that, I have no real skills, however, I do have great ability. The things that others consider to be great that I do, come not from me, but instead they manifest through me.

My intentions are now as follows:

When I see a need, I will find a resource to fill it.

When I see others in fear, I will be fearless as an example for them.

When I observe inspired leadership, I will follow it.

When I observe a lack of leadership, I will take the lead.

When I hear words of wisdom, I will listen to them.

When I am given good advice, I will take it.

When someone shows competency and the conviction to do something, I will endeavor to empower them.

When someone drops the ball, I will pick it up.

When someone's vision is blinded, I will become the eyes that help him or her to see.

When I receive a complaint, I will look at it as a gift, and I choose not to let my ego get in the way of that gift, as the complaint allows me to see if what I am doing works or if it needs modification.

When I find someone who can do something better then I can, I will step back and let him or her do it.

When I look around and see that no one walks with me, I will realize that I am not a leader.

When I see that I have not empowered others to become masters, I will realize that, I am neither a leader nor a master.

Conrad Cain

Blueprints for Living

Heather J. Clarke

*I*n my opinion, beliefs about the world, and ourselves, are formed unconsciously. Once you learn how they are formed, you can, with practice, become the creator of what you desire in life. Beliefs are nothing more than a series of perceptions that we hold to be true based on the meaning we have applied to them from past experiences. Each perception is like a leg on a table. When we group enough perceptions together, a belief is formed. Sometimes, others will gladly add as many legs to that table as possible to help form your beliefs. Beliefs can either free us or imprison us.

We wear our beliefs like a pair of sunglasses that filter possibilities, in or out. Some filters will allow only a narrow band of possibilities to occur in our life. Perceptions form beliefs and create our filters of outward experience.

If we could more consciously examine the way we think, we'd learn that most of what we believe in is formed arbitrarily and based on past experiences. You have made the event, thing or person meaningful. The event, in and of itself, is just an event. However, we apply meaning to the event, and then it becomes real to us.

Instead of living bound to the past, we must live with a sense of expectancy, which can fill us with such happiness. If you practice conscious awareness, you can create abundance without having events themselves drive your feelings. Often what we expect in life is what we experience and, consequently, some people try not to expect too much in case they get their hopes up and are disappointed. Our thinking energy can be used to shape what we see and experience. So where does this energy come from?

What internal dialogue or messages do you repeat to yourself each day? What tapes do you play over and over again in your mind? What kind of inner dialogue do you have with yourself about how you look, how prosperous you are, your state of health, your relationships with friends, family and lovers?

For me, living in the moment is all about being devoted to the balance between my mind, my body and spirit--my positive faith and beliefs about the world. Living in rhyme is working with intent and purposefulness with my beliefs to produce the coincidences and synchronicity in my life.

As a professional working with clients who have disabilities, I align myself with the law of abundance and synchronicity as guiding tools in my practice, while still working within my clients' perceptions and beliefs.

Most clients' belief about their disability is often flavored, and shaped, by their experiences with medical and insurance systems geared toward treating disability as a puzzle to solve or a thing to fix. A disability also has to be understood in context with the individual and their personal story to set the stage for healing and transformation as a precursor to their consideration of alternate careers.

Clients are often surprised when they examine their beliefs through a reframing exercise, in which I help them develop other visions for their lives and find possibility and undiluted potential to draw from. Just like that perception exercise in which you can choose to see in the same picture either a vase or two people sharing an intimate kiss, I help clients refocus their awareness and perception of their medical conditions to mean other things. They begin to see beyond this. The "Ah-ha!" experience when the light bulb comes on—where they had never seen things quite in that light before—is a paradigm shift that transcends the moment. Clients' attitudes about their disabling condition and what is possible for their lives no longer needs to delay their recovery. Now it can transform them.

Using these blueprints to living can transform anyone's life. Applying these basic life principles consistently can make a considerable difference in consciously creating the life you envision. So many distractions from the outside world compete for our attention and make it seem like we have no control over things. That, however, is merely an illusion. Living is so much easier when you know what you read in papers and see on television does not bind you.

Heather J. Clarke BCS., M.Ed., RRP

People: The Secret of Life
Mary Boehmer

I am 20 years old and I truly believe that I have found the secret to true happiness in life. I have found the key to constant laughter, great stories and unlimited joy. All things great, all things that are love and happiness stem from one thing—people.

My life is new and different and filled with such wonderful moments because of the people in my life. I truly believe that the key to success lies within you and the people who come in and out of your life. I believe that the seven most important words are, "Hi, my name is Mary, what's yours?" And through those seven words comes a world of never-ending possibilities. I surround myself with the people who make my life that much better.

My family and my friends are my everything. They have made the story of my life.

Relationships with the people you care about are the key to living the life you want. They comfort you, teach you new things and bring you fun and endless entertainment. Relationships help you to grow and challenge you to be the best person you can be. When you really love someone, and they love you back, life is perfect. And you know that if your life is filled with people who are your everything, then you have everything, every day of your life.

At a very young age, I realized what one person can mean to you. I realized that the people in your life are all that truly matters. Not money, jobs, houses, vacations or what you shot on the back nine. Ask anyone who has had a loved one die.

My dad died suddenly at 42, when I was only 12 years old. This past spring my 17-year old brother died. Their deaths continue to be the greatest challenges I ever faced. But it taught me that spending time with people you love will always bring you happiness.

When someone you love dies, the people in your life replace the pieces of your heart. Since the deaths of my dad and brother, I live my life with passion and enormous gratitude for the gift of life. I love life because I love the people in my life. It is that simple.

Fill your world with people you love to be around and your life will be a true success. You'll wake up each morning unable to wait to talk to the people you love, tell them jokes, watch movies with them, go on trips and vacations with them and take great hilarious pictures with them.

When I grow up and have a house of my own, I want to cover it with pictures of the people in my life. I want black-and-white photographs and bright vibrant colored photographs. I want my walls to be filled with quotes about people, life, love, and happiness. Most importantly, though, I want my house to be filled with the people I love, for all the days of my life.

Mary Boehmer

The Power of Hypnosis
Valerie Davidson

I had heard of hypnosis only in the movies until I was introduced to it in 1982, during a time when my life had reached a crisis, from which it looked like I would never recover. Then a student suggested hypnosis.

I bought a book on self-hypnosis and went off to convalescence for two weeks. I studied for a full week, then practiced it for another three days. That was the first time I had slept without pills in ten months. Just six weeks later, I was back at work. I got on with my life and put hypnosis to the side.

Three years later, I had an accident and was unable to do my job, so I decided to go back to my place of birth. I bought a few properties upon returning home and rented them out. My life was not all roses, but I was quite happy.

Then I began to let stress enter my life. I allowed people to tell me how to live. Before I knew what had happened, I found myself in a psychiatric hospital, on prescription drugs for several months. After my release, I continued as a basket case for over three years.

One day I saw an ad for hypnotherapy, so I made an appointment. That was the start of my recovery.

Hypnotherapy began to help me get my confidence back. Then I put my name on a mailing list and received information on a small gadget that stimulated alpha waves, which I knew hypnosis did. I used it every day. Within six months, I no longer needed prescription drugs.

Then I received information on a new way to meditate. Since I had done it in the past, I knew that meditation stimulated the brain and altered your brainwave patterns. Two years into meditation, I no longer wanted to be a property owner. Stress was still in my life, but it no longer affected my happiness—which was now constant, even though I was receiving no rent from my tenants and was heading for bankruptcy. I began to take charge of my life.

With little money to pay a solicitor, I took another course of hypnotherapy to get my confidence to take a tenant to court for non-payment of rent. A good man in the council helped me prepare a case to defend myself. Then it was back for hypnotherapy to get my courage to face the ordeal alone. It worked!

I won my case. The court instructed the bailiffs and police to repossess my house. My other tenants then realized that I had recovered my spirit, and they left the rest of my properties.

A caring broker managed to get me a small mortgage, and friends got the properties into a sellable condition, so that they sold very quickly. I was able to pay off my debts and refurbish my home.

I thanked God and asked for guidance on my path. Then I woke up to realize I wanted to help others find their own paths to freedom. I have started a course on hypnosis to get a degree and become a therapist myself. When I get my diploma, I can have my own hypnotherapy practice and help others heal their pain and find true happiness, as I did.

Valerie Davidson

The Ultimate Prize

Lorrie Rivers

*I*t all started out with a water cooler. At least, that's what I wanted to think. That it happened because of some random collision of time and place and alignment of Venus in the fourth house and, well, the water cooler.

There was a voice in my right ear asking me to bring the cooler to the tent for the actors. A voice which spoke directly into my brain and I often mistook for God, though it was only a walkie talkie headset. I looked over at my superior and saw him pointing at an enormous icebox full of various chilled liquids, which everyone needed plenty of, being on the beach in South Carolina's summer. It was already 103 degrees and not even noon yet.

I began half carrying, half dragging this behemoth of a water cooler 20 yards to the tent. My heart had already been beating like a crazed butterfly all morning and there were various other strange things going on in my body, but at one point the world started doing strange things as well. The regular, run of the mill, everyday beach sand turned into the sloppiest of quicksand. With each step my foot was being sucked down further and further and was harder and harder to get out. And it wasn't just the sand that had transformed. The sounds around me became very slow and magnified, like I was in a large, cavernous chamber where time was eking out at intervals.

I don't remember setting the cooler down, but I must have because the next thing I knew, I was on a stretcher with a large needle in my arm, hooked up to various beeping machines. And the cooler was nowhere in sight.

From that day on, my life changed indescribably. I went from running five miles a day to barely being able to make it out of my bed to go to the bathroom. I was in pain constantly. I had bouts of paralysis. I was 24 years old and often had to be fed by my father. I couldn't think, I couldn't breathe, it hurt to move and I didn't want to live. And when I was finally diagnosed, it was with Chronic Fatigue and Immune Dysfunction Syndrome, an illness for which the medical community says there is no cure, in fact, for which there is no reliable treatment. I might get better, I might not. I might have this thing for the rest of my life.

Before I became ill, I was always reaching, striving, struggling towards some goal. I often reached those goals but they were hollow. It wasn't enough and I wasn't enough. Everything was difficult and I didn't enjoy my life. It was hard and I was hard on myself and on my body. I thought you must struggle and work yourself really hard. At some point in my illness I realized that if I was going to get out of this thing, if I was going to live my life, the one I'd always wanted to live, then I had to love myself. I had heard it all my life, but what did it mean? I had to figure it out. I finally figured out that it means that you are a beautiful, powerful, special, deserving creature. Not because of something you've done, how you look, what others think of you or how you measure up, but because you exist. You are worthy of whatever it is you want because you are here. And this is what turned things around for me: We are here for the purpose of joy. A phenomenal concept, and one that was especially hard for me to grasp since I'd somehow gotten it into my head that I had to prove myself and my worthiness with sweat, blood and tears.

I'd heard the statement "it's all about the journey, not the destination for years," but never really understood it. After hearing and allowing myself to believe that my purpose in life is to experience joy, the whole "journey" things started to make sense. And gradually, a new world began emerging for me in fits and starts. I would walk outside and, instead of worrying about whether or not I would be able to make it around the block, I'd stop in my tracks, astonished at the delicious brightness of a riot of blooming flowers. I began really loving my body and loving the healing and unfolding process. Loving the sometimes still-painful experience as if it were the most precious, most amazing process I could ever be a part of. Because it is. And now I'm running and singing again. I'm producing a documentary and writing. I help others who are dealing with illness to move toward health and happiness using the same methods I used to get there. People keep asking me if "I'm back to where I was before I got sick." I am and so much more because it is now with spontaneous laughter, mischief and an appreciation for the process of living, the process of being and the process of achieving goals through joy. And that's what it's all about, loving the feeling, the action and life. It's about the journey to get the prize and not the prize itself. Scream your joy! Live your joy! Breathe it, taste it, feel it, every moment. When you do this, the universe answers your happy yells with happy circumstances and success. They're raining down on me even now.

Lorrie Rivers

Wake up... Live the Life You Love, Living on Purpose

Dreams Do Become True

Jose M. Baltazar

My dad and I have had serious conversations since I was a little child. When I was fourteen years old, we'd gone to the store for groceries. When we got home, he parked his truck in front of our house and said he wanted to talk to me. This was going to be one of those conversations.

"Son," he said, "you are already in high school and I am very happy about it. I hope you graduate and go on to college. I want you to get an education. I want you to study for some profession where you won't have to spend the whole day on your knees picking berries, or bending down cutting lettuce, like me."

"Some people work in packing sheds, and the jobs there are a little easier, but even that is hard work. I want you to have an office job or a trade that will be easier for you. Even better, so that you can have your own business. Learn English and stay in school. If I knew English, I could have a grocery store here, as I did in Mexico. When you have your own business, you don't have to work for anybody else."

I clearly remember my reply to him that evening. It came out without premeditation. "Dad," I told him, "I plan to have my own business. But first, I want to go to college and work in computers. I won't work in the field of computers forever, just until I become the manager of a computer center. I will manage it for about five years or so, then I want to be a teacher for a while and help Hispanics get an education. And after I do that for a few years, then I'll go into business for myself."

Now, looking back thirty-eight years later, I see that two-thirds of that dream has unfolded exactly as I told my father. And I know now the last third is coming to fruition. Now, I know that the new dreams I have developed will come true because my past has taught me so.

In 1974, after graduating with a degree in computer science from Hartnell Community College, I got my first job as a computer operator there. Through promotions, and by furthering my education, I became the manager of the computer center in 1982, becoming involved through the college and the church in promoting education and recruiting Hispanics into college. After teaching bi-lingual computer courses for a while, I developed a strong interest in becoming a full-time teacher and counselor. I got my masters and, in 1988, was hired by El Paso Community College as a Counselor and Instructor.

I love what I do and have been doing this job for the past 16 years with the same level of excitement as when I started. I have been happy and fulfilled in my professions. When I left the computer field, I was offered a higher position, but knew it was time to move on. In my present career, I have made a significant positive difference in many of the students I came in contact with.

For your dreams to become true, you need to create what Dr. Wayne Dyer calls a positive intention. This intention needs to be connected to someone or something very meaningful in your life—someone or something with whom you feel a very strong connection, so that when you state your intention, your mind will record it. Your mind will then move you in that direction, even without your awareness. Identify your desires and turn them into intentions by stating them to someone important to you.

My mom and dad were unselfish. My dad would give his lunch to less fortunate coworkers without expecting any payback. He would give part of his crop pick for the day to slower workers who tried to keep up but couldn't, though it meant he would earn less money. My mom would buy new shoes for less fortunate neighbors, as long as ours were still in good shape. I learned this value from my parents and have practiced it in all my endeavors. In my careers, I always have taught about what I do in terms of helping others, or making life easier and more successful for them. Whatever you do, do it to serve others, focusing on how what you do helps others improve their lives.

I've always sought to do my best for my customers and my employers with an attitude of service first. My careers have been very prosperous.

I've learned that, to live a happier and more fulfilled life, you need to let your imagination fly and let dreams come to mind. The dreams that become recurring thoughts are the ones to follow. Listen to and follow your intuition. Make plans and even write them down. Set goals, objectives, and deadlines as conventional wisdom says, but realize that these are only guidelines. Don't make your plans your religion. Allow God to do things His way, and at His time. All you need do is create the intention and state it to someone to whom you feel very connected. I've also learned that stating them to God, who gives you those dreams, creates the strongest intentions. Once you state the intention, do your work unselfishly, with the intention of being the best at it; and your dreams will turn into reality.

Jose Baltazar

Another medicine

Sharon Morrow

*O*ne moment in timelessness is what it takes, one powerful splinter of recognition. Suddenly, the wall separating you from your full potential thunders down into a mountain of past historical patterns and a colorful tapestry of trauma-drama, to be sorted, organized and balanced in conscious understanding. A new horizon is exposed.

All previous limitations to thought, feeling and imagination wink out in that moment and new, exciting frontiers are brought forth into clarity through realizations, people and tools never before encountered. A new life is birthed from the ashes of the dying you have been doing your whole life thus far. Like the Phoenix it will rise again and on colorful wings take you to your divine self and the higher vibrations that create heaven on Earth.

That is truly what happened to me and continues to happen as I accept the mystery of life unfolding. Each timeless moment I create and each "now" that I accept fully and completely, without fear of past or future, brings living the life I love into reality. But, let us go back to the "moment in timelessness."

In 1998 I was a registered nurse in a busy, high-tech, intensive care unit when I began to experience glimpses of the powerlessness I had fostered in my life and in my patients. The truth suddenly became clearly evident, that most of the patients suffered more from the treatments administered by physicians and nurses in hospitals than were healed or helped by them. Tremendous conflict weighed heavily upon me as to whether I was helping or causing further harm to my patients through modern medical techniques. My conflict became so acute that I went to my MD and requested a leave of absence for post-traumatic stress so I could get some space in which to reevaluate my chosen profession. At the same time, a newspaper advertisement about the grand opening of a holistic healing center led me to the metaphysical community. I became one of the center's first students.

It is amazing to me that angels, fairies and magic could be accepted as more healing than the drugs, surgeries, diagnostic procedures and the technological advances of a modern hospital. One belief system offers unlimited possibility and potential. Its success is based on overcoming fear, looking at the whole person, having faith in oneself and in a power greater than oneself. The other system inspires dependency, fear and is motivated by money. This system, our modern health care system, focuses its very narrow vision on disease and symptoms without regard for individual differences, the whole person or the causes of the imbalances. I watched my patients suffer through treatments that left them completely debilitated, maimed physically, spiritually and emotionally with little hope of recovery from the treatments much less the diseases. The introduction of a spiritual dimension and energies refreshed my enthusiasm for life in general. I was introduced to simple, yet effective, tools for healing the causes of disease and imbalances through nutrition, energy medicine, crystals, music, meditation, Chinese herbal medicine, massage, quantum physics, channeling, theta healing, medical intuition and so much more.

Then one moment in timelessness a phone call came as a totally unexpected gift to fully validate my new way of thinking and being, as well as to disconnect me fully from the system I was still attached to in significant ways. "Sharon," my friend said, "I have just spoken to a man they call the Crystal Keeper, and he asked me if I knew someone named Sharon. I said I did, and he told me to tell you as soon as possible that if you don't re-contract with the Universe to get your lessons from living instead of dying, and if your family and friends don't re-contract with the universe to get their lessons from your living instead of your dying, you will be riddled with cancer in six months." I was too stunned to think about how crazy it might be that a man hundreds of miles away, whom I had never met, should care to warn me that my very life in human form was in peril. But I knew he was right; I was aware I had a tumor in my left breast, though I was in denial of its true meaning. I had been protecting myself from conscious awareness of its threatening presence for several months as it grew and became more painful each moment.

I went to see my MD to confirm a fast growing, aggressive cancer. He wanted to schedule a visit with a surgeon the next day, however, I looked at him and stated emphatically, "I grew this, I will un-grow it!" He said, "I will believe in God if you do!"

I went back a year later with the tumor almost completely gone and held him to his word.

When I walked out of my physician's office, I walked out of the world I knew and completely immersed myself in the mysteries of a way of life never experienced before, unlimited and constantly unfolding. I made the simple request to the universe, "Bring me the tools, the knowledge, and the people I need to heal from this cancer and in all ways," and it was so.

I know that my healing journey is not about healing myself from cancer. It is about the intrinsic spiritual re-birthing inspired by cancer. To be asleep and then to be awakened by first a nudge, then a slap and finally a splash of freezing cold water, is sometimes the necessary steps to opening your eyes to your destiny and your sacred contract. And once your eyes are open in every way, you can never go to sleep in the same way again nor dream the same dreams. You are now a conscious being. You can step into your power in a personal connection to your divine higher awareness and self and begin creating, each moment by timeless moment, the life you love to live with purpose.

Sharon Morrow, RN, CMT

The Authentic Self

Elizabeth Eichenbaum

*M*any of us have at least one defining moment in our lives that inexorably changes us forever. Mine took place at age twenty-two in an astrology class. At the time, I was confused about what I was going to do with my life, but I felt something inside pushing me to grow. Fear of change, however, and lack of confidence, sustained a stronger hold on my consciousness. It was a daily, inner struggle.

It's funny how the universe brings you what you need, at the perfect time that you need it. The first day of class, I found myself easily assimilating the vast body of meanings, methods and systems of astrology. I was amazed at my mind's almost effortless integration of this information.

The greatest discovery that day was the realization of how astrology can be used to uncover one's innate abilities and natural strengths. I realized I had a powerful tool, one that could give me, in one hour, more knowledge about the inner workings of my psyche than a therapist could give me in a year. A profound sense of joy overcame me at that moment, as I was able to transcend the limited picture I had of myself. A flood of new possibilities poured into my consciousness along with a passionate desire to know more about astrology and how to use it for personal development.

Since that moment my enthusiasm for astrological insight and how it can be a powerful channel for personal growth inspired me to become a professional astrologer. It is my life's purpose to help people create infinite possibilities for themselves. Many people that come to me are seeking a greater purpose in life. As a consulting astrologer, I work with my clients to uncover the divine message in their horoscopes, which often opens new possibilities—never considered before.

The beauty of astrology insight is the profound shift in self-awareness. The astrological birth chart, which is the alignment of planets at the exact moment of birth, is a comprehensive holistic system that describes your unique personality patterns and your innate strengths and weaknesses. Most importantly, the symbolic language of your birth chart can be used to interpret your life's purpose and provide empowering and life enhancing direction. It is an excellent framework to connect to the ideals of your higher self—the authentic self.

How do you recognize your authentic self? The inner voice that urges you to find meaning and to grow from your life experiences is the unmistakable mark of the authentic self. If you live in alignment with your authentic self, there is nothing you can't achieve. Surrender to the wisdom of your innervoice; allow it to be your divine guide. This is the key to living your life with purpose.

Elizabeth Eichenbaum

Virtual Enchantment
Brad Werner

*F*ive years ago I traveled just about every week teaching computer, networking and security classes in different venues. New students and topics kept my consulting, training and software development company exciting. Life seemed good; I thought that I was happy.

Then I had a vision, a warning flare to wake up! I experienced several major unplanned life changes, such as the departure of my business partner and girlfriend. After acknowledging these changes, with some crying to go along, I made a decision. I pulled the keyboard out of the closet and "wasted" a day playing piano. At the end of the day, I made a CD of the tracks I'd laid down using the PowerBook and the free sequencer software I'd never before taken out of the box. It was an amazing spark, even if my music was amateurish. My decision was not to become a professional musician, but just to take the time to play. From that point on, new possibilities seemed to appear all the time (they've been there all along) yet now I've opened up my heart and eyes so that I'm willing and able to see them.

Music was the seed and spark. As I started writing poetry for the first time in years I began to reconnect with friends and family with whom I'd become distant. I practiced listening and empathizing with others through training toward becoming a Reiki Master/Teacher and ordained minister. Rekindling neglected interests as I started attending Yoga, Tai Chi and meditation classes at a local health food store. These helped me find myself, my center and brought rapid closure to old issues. I felt ready to begin anew and I met many interesting people through these new facets of my life. Most surprisingly I met a beautiful young lady whom I could swear I'd met a thousand times before. We were engaged, in 2001, in a beautiful tropical garden and married in 2003 overlooking the ocean.

Meanwhile I was still traveling and teaching classes all over the United States. But this was taking me away from family - especially a little boy who needed to be with his new dad. I missed telling him bedtime stories and tucking him in.

Then the opportunity presented itself to teach a virtual class. I was quite cynical and doubtful of the practical value of delivering 35 hours of technical training live over the Internet each week. But I also feared that I would be unable to keep their attention for even an hour. I'd become very dependent on physical comedy and dynamic stage presence - how would I keep the audience engaged when I couldn't see them? I was drowning in fear, uncertainty and doubt. I just didn't believe in my ability, and the comfort of the students, to communicate effectively in a virtual classroom.

This was really scary: a virtual room full of people. Yet I had absolutely no idea if they were playing solitaire, staring at their headsets, calling for a refund or maybe listening, getting it and thinking of questions. So I tried something highly technical. I closed my eyes, reached out with Reiki, sent healing energy, meditated on sharing and prayed that this could be better than face to face training. All I had to do was believe. I started to be able to feel or sense what the students were experiencing. Now that I've taught over 50 weeks of classes live online and had many repeat students and rave reviews, it's probably safe to say that I'm not afraid anymore.

One way that I'm living the life I love is spending some time every day the Self in meditation, myself and my family. This helps to make manifest the rest. With the example of the virtual classroom I learn more each day. As I trust the power of intention to right my sails and steer my rudder on this sea of infinite possibilities, I am ever amazed.

Four years ago I'd focused so much on work that none of these daily joys were possible. I'd squeezed out all these amazing possibilities. When I woke up, the possibilities started to open up, to practically burst forth, like flowers opening in February.

Best of all: the flowers appear to be perennials! All I had to do was open my heart and believe in the infinite possibilities.

Brad Werner

Balinese White Magic:
YellowBamboo.com
Alvin Donovan

*T*oday, I certainly do live the life I love, but it was not always so.

At one point, I was known as one of the top speakers/consultants in the world. I had a best selling book *Make More Money NOW* and was considered by many to be one of the most successful people imaginable. I was featured on over 1,500 radio and TV programs and was a faculty member of many of the world's largest management institutes. I consulted for the top CEO's of the Fortune 500 companies.

Yet, there was something missing in my life. After my wife discovered she was seriously ill, we ditched it all to move to paradise. We bought a piece of land on a deserted beach in Bali and built our dream home. Thankfully my dear wife recovered fully. In Bali I am living the kind of life most people only dream, surfing the big perfect world-class waves of the Indian Ocean which I have all to myself.

In Bali I discovered the unlimited power of Balinese White Magic or YellowBamboo.com, as it is known here. YellowBamboo.com is truly the most powerful form of personal development known to humankind and we have over 30,000 practitioners here. The main goals of YellowBamboo.com are personal development, healing and protection.

I became the first Westerner to be certified to teach YellowBamboo. com and now have devoted my life to help others use this technology. I was a yoga and meditation teacher for over 20 years and even ran an ashram in San Diego. The thing that always bothered me about yoga was that the goal was supposed to be self-realization, but in all those years I never saw anyone go from being "normal" to self-realized.

Well, with YellowBamboo.com, it is totally different. You can develop more in one month than with 10 years of yoga or meditation. It actually is that powerful. Yes, I know a lot of people have done the fire walk and think it is a big deal. Many people are now looking for the next big thing.

With YellowBamboo.com you develop so much personal power it is actually possible to knock down others from 10 meters away and heal others of serious illnesses. We have many videos of this happening at the YellowBamboo.com website. Walking on fire means you can control what is going on inside of you, but the YellowBamboo.com power allows you to control what is going on outside of you as well. That is real personal power!

The thing I enjoy most about living the life I love is that the tool of the free video instruction at YellowBamboo.com allows me to bring about rapid and substantive change in my students' lives.

Now my mission is to bring this to the western world by finding others who want to be able to teach their students the unique power of Balinese White Magic.

Alvin Donovan

Soul Affair

Janice Froats

*I*t's been said that every master was once a disaster. Nearly a year ago, as I heard these words for the first time, they resonated deeply with me and held great promise. My life was in shambles, and I was an emotional wreck. Yet the faint whisper of my soul told me there was a higher purpose for my pain.

I had recently separated from my husband, was caring for my two toddlers and was pregnant with a married man's baby. Upon learning of the pregnancy, the man, whom I loved deeply, decided to turn his back on his unborn child and remain with his wife. I contemplated having an abortion or giving up my children. Suicide haunted my despairing and grief stricken mind.

When the pain became more than I could withstand, I fell to the floor and asked for God's help. I prayed for guidance, wisdom and courage to see this experience as a blessing that would someday touch the lives of others. I allowed my life to be divinely guided by spirit, and, in that moment, I had my first lesson in spiritual surrender. My life changed, because my perception changed. I took full responsibility for utilizing these circumstances as an opportunity to grow, mature spiritually and to love.

Rather than choosing to be a victim of life, I prayed that I might be able to see the situation from God's perspective, who undoubtedly has a better understanding than I of why things happen. I began to look for the gifts given to me by each person whom I felt had hurt or betrayed me.

Instead of continuing in feelings of anger and resentment toward my married lover, I had tears of gratitude for his help in transforming me. He was an angel in disguise who cracked my heart wide open, taught me to love, helped me see the beauty within myself and showed me that everything we seek is inside of us. He gave me myself, the greatest gift of all. He was a catalyst for my discovery that we, including myself, are an expression of God. With this awareness, we can heal the world.

My pain was a doorway to discovering my purpose, which is to awaken others to their true and divine selves. I lead seminars, coach people on the spiritual purpose of relationships and on raising spiritually aware children. My passion is to inspire people to challenge the limiting beliefs that keep us small; that send us to seek on the outside what can be found only on the inside.

This journey is not for the weak at heart. It requires patience, courage, strength, trust and perseverance. You will need to be brave to listen to your inner wisdom, and stay true to yourself no matter what. It will be worth it as you discover that you already are all you were ever looking for: peace, harmony, joy and love.

Janice Froats

The Science of 'Living the Life you Love' with Purpose

Tom Leigh, CMH, C.hyp., P.NLP

*B*orn into a large family in 1941, and growing up in north England in postwar poverty, affected me greatly.

I knew my father as an angry man, my mother as a silent, bewildered and withdrawn woman and my life one of religion.

With the cotton mills closing one after another, my father, forced out of his skilled work and standing in long dole queues, had with difficulty, to swallow his pride. I remember him tramping the streets desperately seeking the few unskilled labor jobs available, often holding down three part-time jobs simultaneously.

With no one with the time or patience of whom to ask questions, I took to asking them of myself. God fascinated me until one day, around age 13; I was devastated by something in the sermon that seemed totally wrong.

As we filed out of the church, I tremblingly questioned the minister on what I had heard. The reply shook me still further, "No son, only people have souls."

Having intuitively believed that soul was within everything—the earth, sky and all of life, suddenly the world looked even grayer.

No longer believing in what they taught, I stopped going to church. Yet, still seeing soul in everything, slowly the world came alive again for me, and I began to search further.

Driven by a confusing half-knowledge that I had lived before, I studied many religions, finding many which agreed with my own vision.

I became convinced that all things are individual parts of an indivisible energy we call "spirit." Now I know that the balance between the two opposite poles of that energy result in creation and destruction, success and failure, love and hate; but knowing this we can consciously choose for ourselves what it is to be.

Finding scientific proof of my findings, I published my Internet course, The Cosmic Net, so that those who are as lost as I was can find confirmation of their own intuitions. The result is freedom of mind, the cure of stress, then health and success.

It was an extraordinary and exciting discovery that the mind, body and brain make up a "dipole gate," and that through the gate of ourselves, the vast and inexhaustible spirit-energy of the vacuum can be channeled at will. This explains, scientifically, how 'faith' healers effect their healing and psychics span time and distance with their thoughts. We all do this subconsciously of course, or we could not live at all. Now I find we can learn how to do it consciously, for health, success and the resolution of negative 'cause and effect', or "karma."

Understanding now why my life happened with those particular circumstances and people, I knew also that karma is one of 'The Psyche Energy Linking" of the thought-energy of all minds, that what we think and do is the force that creates time, and so the future we will later experience.

By not meekly accepting the cant of others, but by actively asking questions within the silence of our own minds, we can alter what our futures will be and so move forward, opening up our psychic senses to actively *evolve* ourselves mentally and spiritually. The future is ours; we don't have to merely accept: we can, "Wake up and live the Lives we Love with Purpose."

Tom Leigh, CMH, C.hyp., P.NLP

The Power of a Mastermind in Pursuit of Your Purpose

Jenya Hampton

"You'll never make it. You don't know anything about that business!" I've heard these words every time I started a new business. And every time, the person who uttered those words ended up eating them.

Now, don't get me wrong; I am not an egomaniac, nor do I pretend to know everything. As a matter of fact, I'll be the first to admit I know that I don't know. But that's never stopped me from pursuing my purpose of growing, learning, trying new things and helping people along the way.

The key to my success in the industries that I once knew nothing about was, and still is, surrounding myself with people who share my vision and possess the knowledge that I do not.

Today, just about every good business and "how-to-succeed" book includes the advice to surround yourself with people who share a common goal, who possess excitement and vision, who are upbeat and positive. This last factor is the key: who support you in the quest for your dream.

In his book *Think and Grow Rich*, Napoleon Hill called this group of supporters a mastermind. I cannot overstate the importance of a mastermind group as it relates to success in business. All of us have negative influences in different areas of our lives. These are typically people who have given up on their own dreams, or never had enough belief in themselves to even consider the option of bringing their dreams to life. These people affect us only to the degree to which we allow them.

When it comes to pursuing your dream, however, it is vital to eliminate or minimize any negative influences. For your dream to survive its fragile early stages, you must be able to share your most precious ideas with someone else who believes in you and your ability to succeed. Articulating your dream to someone for the first time makes you very vulnerable to the feedback. When you know that you're in a supportive, understanding environment, this first revelation can fuel you with excitement and the power to take the first steps to actualizing your dreams. As you start experiencing successes along the way, you will become less susceptible to the negativity of others, because of the strengthening of your belief in yourself.

There are examples of mastermind groups throughout history; the most famous being Jesus and the Apostles. Today's most familiar examples of mastermind successes are people like Bill Gates, Oprah Winfrey and the President of the United States; all of whom achieved their success because of unwavering self-belief, commitment to their goals and the support, and idea sharing, of their mastermind groups.

In a recent interview, Bill Gates stated that he schedules time to brainstorm with the heads of all the divisions of his company everyday. He went on to say that this is one of his most important activities for the future growth and survival of his company. Oprah Winfrey brainstorms with a group that includes subgroups of her viewers, who share their feedback and ideas. The President has cabinet members, personal staff and his father, who brings first-hand experience to the job. The President consults with all of these people before any major decision or action is put into place. Our founding fathers knew the power of a mastermind when they designed the Constitution. Can you imagine what it would be like if the President of the United States made all his decisions alone?

Recently, I decided to introduce the idea of a mastermind group into every new and existing business as a vital part of their business plan. Today, more and more people are following their passion and going into business for themselves. Yet the rate of business failure is continuing to go up too. I believe there are two reasons for this: under-funding and lack basic business skills. I can't do anything about the first reason, but I believe that knowing how to set up a mastermind group, and finding the right people to support you, can solve the second. I introduced this idea to my mastermind group, and as a result of their support and understanding of my vision, they have helped me reach a mass audience as I develop a company to bring this vision to businesspeople all over the world.

Whether you're already in business, pursuing your passion, or just in the idea stage, I urge you not to shortchange yourself in the process. Find and develop people who will support you in your pursuit. Become part of a mastermind!

Jenya Hampton

Wake up... Live the Life You Love, Living on Purpose

One Door Closes Two More Open
Art Martin

When I graduated from high school, my father pushed me into entering an engineering career since the Sputnik era had just begun. I decided that was not for me after a year and half. Undecided as to where to go from here and knowing that if I did not stay in college, I would lose my deferment; I joined the Navy since I had a two-year obligation from my reserve status.

This was a huge educational step. I discovered nobody cared about you. You were just a number on the roster. I was forced to learn how to be assertive and speak up. This forced learning process opened many doors for me in understanding how to survive in the world.

When I went back to college I shifted my whole objective entering the field of journalism and marketing/advertising. I kept opening new doors by forcing myself to step into areas that pushed my limits Even though it brought up fear I pushed myself stepping into the unknown. I was not aware this was an effort to build my self esteem, self confidence and get validation. I pushed myself into taking public speaking courses and getting on the discussion and debate team. This opened more doors because I was comfortable being in the public eye. I didn't have to force myself anymore. It became a challenge to see how much I could accomplish. I became the advertising manager for the college newspaper, founded a humor magazine and entered student government.

I tried working in the advertising field discovering it was very different in the real world of competition. I tried real estate and stock market as a day trader which was fun but it was not where I wanted to be. When we hit it financially, my wife I decided to investigate new areas to live. We traveled around the world looking for a better location but returned to California deciding that we were already in the best place to live.

We moved to the Napa Valley and bought an abandoned prohibition era winery and rebuilt it. This was not my calling either. We sold it and moved on building restaurant. This was the turning point. I hired a night manager who had been a chemical engineer. My question to him was, "Why do you want to take a $6.00 an hour job with no benefits?" Over the next year we discussed his main reason, to find himself and get on purpose in his life. After a year of discussing this topic every day and reading some of the books he gave me, I sold my restaurant and retired at 41.

The goal was to find my purpose in this life was. This was 1978. I lived with 24-hour back pain and was told by a doctor I would end up in a wheelchair due to deterioration of my spine. Locating the cause of my back pain became my search for my mission. I tried and studied Chinese, Tibetan medicine and over 20 alternative therapies. None revealed a method to alleviate my back pain.

In 1982 I found my mission and purpose after searching for over 25 years. I discovered our mind is a computer, and affirmations are the software to rewrite defective programs. I created a new definition of Energy Medicine and Energy Psychology over the next 20 years. My purpose and passion is to show and teach people you can reclaim your personal power and take control over your life since I was able heal myself. Suffering and struggling are false beliefs. We can live in love, peace, happiness, harmony and joy. We create miracles on demand in my practice daily by reprogramming the minds files. There is an answer for everything from lack of money and success to the common cold, cancer, pain, or illness and disease. The key to success is releasing the defective programs then using desire, intent, determination, commitment, and discipline.

Art Martin

Life by Numbers
Daniel R. Hardt

I have found the work that I love without really knowing what I had been seeking. Since I had no clear-cut goals, I was too easily influenced by the dreams other people held for me. With all the strength of her faith, my mother wanted me to be a minister. My high school chemistry teacher was convinced that my home should be the laboratory. A friend told me that I would be wasting my talents if I didn't practice law.

I arrived at DePauw University with a firm determination to major in chemistry, but it was a determination, not a passion. After I filled the lab with a toxic compound that escaped from an experiment, doubts crept up on me. By the time I got to organic chemistry, I realized that my chosen path would require more than will power.

Instead, with a sociology major and an English minor, I was accepted into the law school of my choice. Then I received an offer to teach at DePauw. They would give me an immediate contract contingent upon successful completion of a higher degree. I love to teach, and I would have been good at it. But I refused the offer in favor of law.

As a lawyer, I maintained an active church affiliation. I was appointed to the Board of the Ministers' Retirement Fund. I was not a minister, but close enough to bring my mother joy. Looking at the church from the top down, the view is quite different from looking up from the bottom. I became disillusioned.

My world crashed. I could not continue with the practice of law. My marriage ended in divorce. I left the church and held a private pity-party. I did not regret the losses, only the lack of direction. My roots were gone. My dreams were uncovered as shams. I was still pursuing someone else's desires.

Over six months of working as a boilermaker, I sweated out the emotion and decided that it was time to move my life forward again. I spent the next twenty years learning to be a salesman, supplemented in slow times with restaurant work. I really enjoyed the manual labor and the restaurant environment, but both inner and outer voices were telling me that I was wasting my talents.

For several years, I was a licensed hearing-aid specialist. Although the position required a certain degree of professional training, it was still a sales job and a difficult one at that. Those who need the product most are often in denial about their hearing loss. Chris, the manager at the office where I was working, was a numerologist. On slow days, we discussed philosophy, theology and metaphysical concepts.

The breakthrough came when Chris began reading my numerology chart, and I could clearly see the patterns of my life. The tortuous journey now made sense. Finally I was able to put all the pieces together. It had taken half a century, but I had finally found the one area I could be passionate about.

With numerology my full time profession now, and with a supportive partner, all the pieces fit. Although not the religion of my childhood, numerology has a strong spiritual base. I am writing consistently, teaching classes and promoting the work. These areas tap into the sales experience and my love of writing. Since a major emphasis of my practice is using numerology as a business tool, those years of legal practice weren't wasted.

Living the life I love is its own reward, and it leads in an ever-expanding direction. We are in the preparation stages for a new business center. The syndication of the weekly radio segment will soon grow to several additional markets, and the subscriber list of the *Daily Numeroscopes* is multiplying. Above all, I am fully alive.

Daniel R. Hardt

From seeking to finding
Jennifer Remling

*I*f you don't know where you are going, it does not matter what road you take. My life's journey has had many twists and turns, and I hope you find it helpful.

In October 2000 I took my dream job as a Director of Recruiting for an e-commerce company in London. This was a big deal for me because I always had the dream of living and working in Europe for which my husband graciously quit his job as an architect. Two weeks after arriving in London, my boss in the United States resigned, then his boss resigned and then they fired the entire recruiting group. There I was in London, my husband had not even arrived yet, and I was concerned about being laid off.

I ended up working there for 6 months and then laid off the entire team when we closed down the office. Meanwhile, my husband got a job with a global architecture firm in London, which offered him a job in San Francisco. We got an apartment in San Francisco, shipped our furniture ahead, and we were going back to Atlanta to wrap up loose ends. The day before we were to move to San Francisco, my husband's company called and told him he no longer had a job because they had lost two major clients and were laying off people.

We decided not to go to San Francisco so I immediately called the moving company and asked them not to send our furniture to San Francisco. They told me the ship had left the port that morning and there was nothing they could do. I had to pay $5,000 to get the furniture to Atlanta, which arrived two months later in a truck that had holes in the top of the trailer. It had rained most of the way and a lot of furniture was ruined. One month later, one of our dogs died tragically, the day before September

11. All of this took place within an eight-month period and it took me five months to find a job in the United States - with a major pay cut.

Believe it or not, I am really glad that I had these experiences because it forced me to take some time and think deeply about life and what it meant to me. I realized that I was probably not on the right path and I started to read books about creating the life you want and connecting with your purpose. Over a two year period I experimented with different business ideas and attended seminars and courses on creating the life that you want.

Then one day I was at a seminar when the speaker said, "There are too many seekers in the world, the world needs more finders." A light bulb turned on; it was time for me get moving and apply what I already knew to be true. That is when things began to change significantly for me. I had financial obligations that I couldn't just walk away from, so I couldn't just quit my job and focus on what I wanted to do. I decided it was time to build a bridge to my dreams, so I really focused on what my dreams were and how I wanted to live my life. I began doing what I wanted to do a little bit every day. Within six months my day mostly consisted of doing just what I wanted to do. I am amazed at how fast it went once I started to apply the techniques and principles I learned. I got business from a colleague that I had worked with in the past that brought in 70 percent of my annual salary in three months. I have used some of that income as investment in my other projects.

Today, I set my own schedule and have time to exercise, write, read and travel with my husband. I feel more free than I have ever felt in my life and it gets better every day. I am certain that my purpose in life is to write and to share what I have learned; to help people build a bridge to their dreams from wherever they are. I have built the bridge; I am well across the bridge. Won't you come with me?

Jennifer Remling

See What You Want

Bill Harris

Until about age 40, I was definitely not living the life I loved. I was chronically angry, often depressed, and had one abysmal relationship after another. I had no real career and no idea how to create one. The direction of my life was down, or, at best, sideways.

This was all a blessing in disguise, though, because it created an intense motivation to learn what happy, peaceful and successful people did that I wasn't doing.

Today, I'm married to a wonderful woman who really loves me. I make ten times what I used to fantasize about. Plus, I have a challenging career doing something I love.

My anger problem is gone, and I haven't been depressed for even a minute in nearly fifteen years.

Now, at age 54, I truly am living the life I love. This transformation happened when I discovered a few key principles that created tremendous positive change for me. They will work for you, too.

What are these secrets?

First, happy people acknowledge that they are creating their reality internally and externally. They see circumstances as an influence but know that what they do inside creates how they feel and behave, and what people and situations they draw to themselves.

For most people, processing external circumstances happens unconsciously. This makes it seem as if circumstances cause your feelings, behavior and what you attract into your life. When this happens, it seems as if you are the effect of external causes over which you have no control.

Happy people, however, even if they can't see how, know they're creating whatever is happening. They take responsibility.

Another characteristic of happy people is that their actions are the result of the possibilities they see. Where the unhappy person sees a challenge as impossible, the happy person sees what is possible. And, by focusing on what is possible, happy people make those possibilities come true.

A third characteristic of happy, successful people: They focus their minds on what they want and keep their mind off of what they do not want.

Take prosperity, for instance. You could focus on not being poor, or you could focus on being rich. That is, you could make a mental picture of poverty, wanting to avoid it, or you could create a picture of being wealthy, wanting to move toward it.

In both cases the intention is the same, but your brain doesn't care about your intention. It just sees the literal content of the picture. When you focus on riches, it thinks you want riches and motivates you to see opportunities, find resources, and take action to be rich.

When you focus on not being poor, it sees a picture of being poor and motivates you to see opportunities, find resources and take action... to be poor.

Most people focus on what they want to avoid without realizing the consequences. When they get what they didn't want, they assume they didn't focus hard enough and redouble their efforts. This creates even more of what they don't want, which creates more frustration.

The other penalty for focusing on what you don't want is that you feel bad. In fact, all bad feelings and negative outcomes are the result of focusing on what you do not want. Instead of unconsciously, and automatically, focusing on what you don't want, consciously and intentionally focus on what you do want. When you do this, you instantly begin to create it, and you instantly feel good.

The final characteristic: Happy people are consciously aware. As a result, their brains are less likely to run on automatic, creating internal states and internal outcomes they did not intend and do not want.

First, become more consciously aware through meditation. Though traditional meditation is very beneficial, at Centerpointe Research Institute we use an audio technology called Holosync to create deep meditative states, literally at the push of a button. This greatly accelerates the meditation process and allows you to create increased conscious awareness very quickly.

Second, investigate your own beliefs, values, ways of filtering information, strategies for decision making, motivations and other internal processes. Centerpointe's Life Principles Integration Process is a structured way of investigating and changing these internal processes, allowing you to take charge of how you create your internal and external results.

There is a price to pay to live the life you love. But paying it is a joyful enterprise which will benefit you for the rest of your life. You create your reality, so learn to focus your mind on what you want and increase your conscious awareness through meditation and self-inquiry.

The life you love is waiting for you!

Bill Harris

Wake up... Live the Life You Love, Living on Purpose

Leaning into Fear.

Richard Metler

*R*ecently I began a process of mind mapping to create some additional income in my life. I giggled at the first thing that came to mind, that I could write a best-selling book. I laughed again and thought to myself, "I can't discount this because it appeared in my thoughts." I came up with a few more ideas and wrote them down. I looked at the computer as I put my pen down, noticing an e-mail had just appeared. In the subject line were the words "Be my co-author." How coincidental was that!

I decided to pursue the e-mail opportunity and agreed to write my story. As soon as I hung up the phone I could feel the fear coming up. It was in the pit of my stomach. What will I write about and what do I have to offer to others? How could I write a book?

Fear can be such a great motivator at times. It can also overwhelm us. I know a great deal about fear. At one point in my life, my fear escalated to panic. In dealing with the panic, I was finally able to see the source of my pain and play through it.

Playing through fear and panic: how is that possible? After living with panic for a little over a year, I finally was so tired of it that I began to make it my friend. I could feel the fear rise from my belly and move up into my chest. If I could be okay with the fear it would subside. I discovered that in accepting the feelings they lost their power. If I resisted, I felt powerless and the fear would escalate to panic.

I thought I had discovered one of the keys to life. All I had to do was be willing to feel the fear and it would dissipate. I really got cocky–and for the next few weeks I was able to live fearlessly. Then my cockiness caught up with me. I noticed that my fear was coming but with more intense energy. It had such a grip on me that I'd never experienced before. In the midst of the feelings of panic I realized the only way through was to feel it fully--to accept it. I leaned into the fear, which

For your free gift, go to: **www.wakeupgift.com**

revealed the source of my distress. I could clearly see all that was happening—and could hear what I was screaming as the events of a traumatic past experience appeared in my mind. I fell to the floor and cried. Then I realized that the panic was gone, and that was the last experience that I've had with panic. That was 11 years ago.

My life has blossomed in so many ways since that day. I have become more spiritual and find myself being more connected with people. I have embraced a life of learning – about others and myself. My finances and financial opportunities have steadily grown and I see myself on the verge of skyrocketing in success. I alone created the fear and panic in my life. I am the one with the power to convert my fear energy into motivational energy. Where will my life go from here? I'm excited at the prospects. My question for you, what do you fear?

Richard Metler

Get a Life: A Journey to the Soul of Your Business

John Jantsch

A popular notion suggests it is somehow healthier to create a clear separation between your business and your personal life. Until you can accomplish this separation, you will become imprisoned by whatever you do to make a living. Just look around, and you will see plenty of evidence to support this claim. It's not hard to find business owners whose businesses have sucked the life right out of them. What they created to give them opportunities for more freedom has imprisoned them. Now they experience little joy in the daily erosion of what was once a bright and shining vision.

But that's just the way it is. That's business! That's why you've got to leave your business and everything to do with it at the door every night, before it takes over the rest of what you have.

What if you started thinking of your business as a vital part of your life? What if this thing that consumes more of your time than anything else became a glorious way to express who you are?

It's entirely possible that any business' primary purpose is to give you, and those who work with you, more life and freedom. The missing ingredient here isn't separation but connection.

For your business to be a source of greater life, first you must understand what more life and freedom really mean to you. What do joy and happiness look like to you, and only you? You need to uncover your unique purpose and connect that purpose to your business; for that is the soul of your business.

Everyone has a unique purpose in life, but, for many people, it has become covered with layers of doubt and fear. Can you remember what led you to start your business in the first place? Reconnecting your business with what your wants, past and present, will allow you to embark on the most important journey you will ever lead.

You can communicate, implement and live your unique purpose when you demonstrate how your business is different, how you plan to influence people and the value of what your business offers in their lives. That is how you communicate, implement and live your unique purpose through your business.

Connecting your life's purpose through your business will then automatically let you attract the clients and opportunities you need to further enrich your life and live your purpose more deeply.

In your search to re-ignite the flame of purpose in your business, let me leave you with three questions, which, if answered honestly, will begin the journey to the soul of your business.

1.   What do you want in your life?
2.   What don't you want in your life?
3.   What are you willing to give up to have the life you want? Don't limit yourself to material things here. Many people need to give up fear of failure or those inner doubts that tell them they are not good enough.

Be patient and keep searching your heart. When you choose to listen to and follow your heart, you will begin to hear the faint strains of harmony, even in the clamor of chaos.

John Jantsch

How I Used Adversity to Find My LIfe's Mission and How You Can Too!

George Stavrou

Section 1: Background

My first long-term relationship of 7 years ended in same year I was disbarred from University for two years. I was only 23. Was there a connection between the two? There certainly was. My second long-term relationship lasted three years and ended at 30 years of age. I worked at unfulfilling jobs and lived at home with my parents. I had over $100,000 in debt and $1,000 a month in credit card interest.

In addition to financial difficulties, I was in poor health, suffering from bouts of depression. At my worst, I had 25 percent body fat and weighed 250 lbs. No wonder my business, as a personal trainer, was suffering. How could I motivate others to get into shape when I couldn't even take care of myself?

Add this to the equation: My father suffers from depression and hasn't worked in over 10 years. Also, I defaulted on a loan co-signed by mother. I owed her about $30,000.

Words like "loser," "hopeless" and "pathetic" may come to mind as you read this. So, I sat down and took a long, hard look at myself to figure out what I wanted to do with my life. Obviously, what I was doing wasn't working.

Section 2: The Present Date

Since then I have become a number one best-selling author on Amazon.com with my first e-book and received the "Player of the Year Award" through the Monthly Mentor program. My debts are half of what they used to be. Filing for bankruptcy was not an option. I filed what is called a "consumer proposal." This is a proposal between me and my creditors stating that I will pay back a portion of what I owe in credit card debt. Something is better than nothing and my credit will be affected poorly for two years after I have paid off what I owe. Filing for bankruptcy would have made things easier for me but I would not have owned up to my contribution to the above.

Section 3: What I've learned along the way

I have learned:

From Coach Ian King's ebook, Paycheck To Passive, I learned:
- work with who I want, when I want, where I want
- set-up systems that will allow me to do this
- leverage myself so that I can help as many people as possible which, in turn, will benefit me

From Robert Kiyosaki and his book "Rich Dad, Poor Dad: What the Rich Teach Their Kids About Money That the Poor and Middle Class Do Not!"

Ten steps to awaken your financial genius
1. I need a reason greater than reality
2. I choose daily
3. choose friends carefully
4. master a formula and learn a new one
5. pay yourself first
6. pay your brokers well
7. be an "Indian giver"
8. assets buy luxuries
9. the need for heroes
10. teach and you shall receive

Section 4 Current Project

"How you Can Sculpt A Leaner, Healthier Body In 12 Weeks!" is my book/ebook/dvd project. This project will take at least the next two years to develop and implement properly as far as setting up systems A LA Robert Kiyosaki, Michael Gerber, etc. Once the systems are in place, I will be financially free and living my life on purpose! Learn more about me and my project through my site www.bodysculpting.ca and sign up for a FREE copy of my ebook.

Section 5: Where I see myself in the future - five years from now

My next goal is to become what Mark Victor Hansen and Robert Allen refer to as an "Enlightened Millionaire." Generally speaking, this is someone that becomes a millionaire to not only help themselves and their loved ones but help society at large.

Section 6: The End of My Journey or is it Just the Beginning?

What is my purpose in sharing my story with you? First, it is to let you know that everyone has their challenges, obstacles and adversities to overcome. Secondly, if you believe in yourself and associate with the right people, especially if you consciously search out powerful mentors, you too will be able to "Wake Up and Live a Life on Purpose"!

Best wishes for you on your own journey.

George Stavrou

Wake up... Live the Life You Love, Living on Purpose

Purposeful, High Quality Questions Lead to a High Quality Life

Dr. John F. Demartini

Could the quality of your life be determined by the quality of the questions you ask yourself daily? The answer is, "Absolutely yes!" Imagine the difference, depending on which of the two following questions you ask. 1. How can I afford to go on vacation? 2. How can I get paid enormously to go on my dream vacation?

The first question leads you to ponder how you can reshuffle your economic resources and valuable time in such a way so as to be able to take time off for a costly vacation. The second question leads you to contemplate how you could actually build your wealth while going on a dream vacation. The former vacation results in a price, the latter in a rewarding dream.

You are probably used to asking yourself the first kind of question and have not even considered the second kind. The former leads you toward living a more quiet life of frustration and desperation. But when you have broken through to another level of questioning you begin to ask yourself more specific, self-actualizing questions, which open the doorway to a more inspired and fulfilling life. For you to live a high quality life you must demand from yourself the answers to high quality questions.

Quality questioning involves a form of deeper self-inspection. Sometimes a whole series of possible answers are required before you come to the one that provides you with the highest quality results. An example of a low quality and high quality question include:

Low-Quality: How come people are so stupid?

High-Quality: What are my customer's motives for buying, and why can't they see the value of my product?

The quality of your life is based partly upon the quality of the questions you ask yourself daily. If you are not inspired by your life, or if you are not living the life you truly dream of, it just may be because you are not asking yourself the highest quality questions. The moment you do is when your life begins to transform. When you are struggling through life, you are asking yourself such uninspiring questions that your life becomes exactly that: uninspiring. Asking yourself low-quality questions leads to a low-quality life, but asking yourself high-quality questions is one of the keys to living the more self-actualized life you dream of and deserve.

There is a bit of thinking involved in asking and answering high quality questions, but with a little effort and refinement you can certainly accomplish a great number of objectives and fulfill a greater number of dreams.

Don't you deserve to live your dreams? Don't you deserve to self-actualize your life?

Now, begin asking yourself quality questions and see to what answers they lead. Be as specific and concise as you can. Watch how your creativity begins to soar. The quality of your life is based partly upon the quality of the questions you ask yourself daily and the quality and quantity of actions you take for yourself daily. Begin to ask higher quality questions and begin to act on your dreams today.

Dr. John F. Demartini

Choice Behavior

Tim Kelley

*I*n the past six months, my life has come into very clear focus. What seemed like a very bizarre series of twists and turns now appears have been a very specific training program. What has made this difference in how I view my life? Knowing my purpose.

Throughout my youth, I was a scientific, inquisitive and skeptical young man. Looking back, I refer to myself during this period as a "sciento-atheist." I looked to Newton, Darwin and Einstein, not the Bible, to explain the world around me and my role in it. I was successful at nearly every endeavor I undertook, and my future seemed clear. I was overjoyed at being accepted to MIT, and I had constructed a clear plan for my life. I would major in electrical engineering, join the Naval ROTC, and become a Marine fighter pilot. I chose the Marines because they had the highest ratio of astronauts relative to their population of pilots. The astronaut program was my real goal.

This plan came to an abrupt end when I could not maintain passing grades in my electrical engineering courses. I was unable to get myself to study, and didn't attend most of my classes. My own behavior didn't make any sense to me, and seemed almost involuntary. I had no choice but to take a leave of absence. MIT was very gracious about my choice and provided me with great support. The Navy was not terribly understanding of my difficulties and shipped me off to swab decks for two years.

It was clear that something was operating in my life that was beyond my control. This made no sense in the scientific, deterministic world in which I lived.

Two years later I finished my tour in the Navy, having become an expert in the dying art of navigation. I returned to MIT and completed a degree in mathematics in only three semesters. I felt as though my life was back on track.

There was one problem, however. The theological and spiritual questions that had merely nagged me as a child were now a thorn in my side. As I moved on to an eight-year career at Oracle Corporation, I was left asking, "Is this all there is?" My clear, scientific world had one flaw: it was a world without meaning, and this left me feeling empty inside.

The twists and turns of my life took me through several years conducting personal growth workshops, and ten years as a consultant and coach. Then something began to change. One night I had a dream unlike any other I had ever had. In complete blackness, a voice spoke: "Your purpose is to help others find their paths." The dream lasted only seconds, and I awoke immediately. The words were burned into my brain. I have never written them down before.

But what did this mean? What did it mean to help people find their paths? I still hadn't found mine! A very insightful friend of mine helped me put it into perspective. "Well, if you're going to guide others along their paths, you're not going to be very well qualified if you find your own too easily."

Since then, my coaching and consulting have taken on an entirely different flavor. Rather than giving people general help on achieving their goals, or offering companies a variety of services to improve their results, I now offer only one service: help in finding one's purpose. In the consulting world of organizational development, this process is called creating a vision. It clarifies exactly where a company wants to go, and creates excitement and buy-in among the employees. It goes beyond a simple business plan or market strategy, as it challenges the organization to answer a deeper question. What principle or purpose drives you?

My coaching practice has changed dramatically. Having fully clarified my own purpose, I find that I can help most of my clients find their life's purpose in about three to five hours of coaching over the span of two to three weeks. Many of them walk away thrilled at this point while some choose to stay on to work on the details of manifesting their newfound purpose.

In retrospect, I am relieved to see that something deeper has been guiding me all along. What seemed like accidents and failures at the time were really shifts in my curriculum. Some call this guiding principle a soul, some call it God, and some call it the unconscious. To me, what matters is that for each of us has a purpose, and each of us has someone or something guiding us along our path.

Tim Kelley

I live with a fighter
Lee Beard

As someone who worked for years in film and television, I can't help but store lessons and images like movies in my mind. Similarly, I find myself drawing on films to help me remember most vividly what really matters to me.

There are two movies that really stir my emotions: *G.I. Jane* (for your family, I recommend the television edited version) and *Rocky III*. Both of these movies involve purpose and determination in two different professions. I saw *Rocky III* first and the story line has always been an inspiration to me.

Everyone is familiar with the story of the Philadephia club fighter who is drifting—along and confused—through an uninspired life. When chance gives him a shot at the world heavyweight boxing championship, his life undergoes an amazing change. Now that he has a definable purpose in his life, his vision of tomorrow improves. His health is restored; his emotions are in control.

His interpersonal relationships are renewed, strengthened, tested and expanded, bringing him new happiness and energy. His faith in himself is restored, and, in the end, he proves himself to be the equal of the best in the world.

As a demonstration of the power of "purpose," that should be enough.

But when the film begins in *Rocky III*, the central character is already a champion. In preparing to retire, he accepts a bout with a "hungry" fighter. Rocky trains like a superstar, without energy or commitment. When the match is held, he is defeated.

An old friend and former champion tries to train him, encouraging him to recover his "edge." They go to the gym where Apollo first trained to try to find that passion and emotion that drove Rocky in the beginning. But, one day, Rocky stops during a training run on the beach.

Apollo concludes: "It's over." He calls out to Rocky, "What's the matter man?" Rocky sadly responds, "I don't want it any more." His once-clear purpose is just as obvious as ever, but it no longer sustains him. What could be wrong?

His quiet wife, Adrienne, reassures him: "If it's over because you want it to be over then I'm glad." However, with persistence, and a few more questions, she finally asks, "What's the truth?" Rocky's frustrated reply is, "I'm afraid!"

Then she says, "We can't live like this, you can't live like this. It's going to haunt you for the rest of your life. You'll always live in fear that someone will take things away from you, that you're not a man anymore. Well, none of it is true. But you, you've got to want it, not for Apollo, not for Mickey, not for the money, not for me, but for you, just you alone."

"And if I lose?" Rocky asks. "Then you lose with no regrets, no fears and I know you can live with that," was her reply. "How'd you get so strong?" asks Rocky. Adrienne's reply: "I live with a fighter!"

I remember a question on an employment examine that asked when I was last in a fight. I thought it was probably junior high school. Then, I realized later that I'm in a fight almost every day. There is always a struggle; I could give up or fight on. I never thought of it as a fight, but it really is a choice of "quit and go home" or "stay and fight."

Often we have to decide. Is it true that "I don't want it anymore?" Or will we decide that this is too important, too much fun or has too much potential to give it up? Knowing your purpose in life is vital; but having the strength and the courage to pursue it is equally important.

I've come to realize that I live with a fighter. C'est moi!.

Lee Beard

Author Index

Buckley, Sian .... Page 11
AFP
Director
Astron Money Managers SA (Pty) Ltd
1293 Church Street,
Hatfield 0083
Pretoria
Gauteng
South Africa
Tel: +27 (0) 12 4307960
Fax: +27 (0) 12 5432769
info@astron.co.za
www.astron.co.za

Cain, Conrad .... Page 55
Conrad Cain lives in Atlanta with his lovely wife.
His first "worldly" discussions of spirituality were with his neighbor and friend
Janice, when they were 6 or 7 years old. They talked about how strange most
people seemed to act in the world. His first introduction to organized reli-
gion as was at the age of twelve when he attended weekly classes at St. Paul's
Episcopal Church. He knew that there was very little personal truth in what
was being taught and that his "other" memories very much contradicted them.
He has now read over 1,500 books looking for something to tie it all together.
He never found another person or book that fully shared his understanding of God until his wife Danna brought home *"Communion with God"*.
As he read it he said to her "you've got to read it too!" She did and she
agreed that was what he'd been saying, but this book clarified it for her.
Conrad wants to no longer be, just an idle observer, but to become an active participant in creating the SHIFT within humanity to embrace a new paradigm of reality. He has learned just how powerful the power of intention can be and that whatever he can truly believe in, that he can achieve. He knows that when one's intentions are in alignment with one's life's purpose, miracles will be manifested daily
Conrad Cain can be contacted at conradcain@bellsouth.net

Clarke, Heather J. .... Page 59
BCS., M.Ed., RRP
Vocational Career Counsellor in the field of rehabilitation, helping people make
new career choices as they transition back to work following downsizing of
a company after an illness/injury. Deemed an expert witness in court
Opened a vocational rehabilitation business in 1997 and eventually incorpo-
rated in May 2001 under the title of Career Innovations Corporation Inc.
Career Innovations Corporation, Inc.
1698 Kingswood Lane, Kingston, NS B0P 1R0
Toll Free: 1-866-441-9991
Telephone: (902) 765-3532
Facsimile: (902) 484-5597
hclarke@careerinnovations.org
www.careerinnovations.org

Wake up... Live the Life You Love, Living on Purpose

The Chopra Center for Well Being
7630 Fay Avenue
La Jolla, CA 92037
Fax: 858-551-9570

29. Grafton road.
Whitleybay.
Tyne &wear.
NE26. 2NR.
0191-290-1039
valerie6188@yahoo.com

Professional speaker, consultant and best-selling author of, How
    to Make One Hell of a Profit and Still Get to Heaven.
john@drdemartini.com
www.drdemartini.com

He is so dedicated to helping others that he gives away FREE materials—He
    offers to all his readers a free two hour Yellow Bamboo training vcd you can
    watch right on your computer. Normally retails for over USD$100 butyou can
    download it right now free at www.yellowbamboo.com or www.bamboovido.
    com. Maija helped me make it. Alvin is looking for those who wish to teach
    this art. For more information email Alvin at info@yellowbamboo.com.
http://yellowbamboo.com
info@yellowbamboo.com

Dr. Erika Duffy holds a Doctorate in C.O.R.E. ™ Education and is a certified Holistic
    Counselor, certified Enneagram Counselor, certified hypnotherapist, certified Life
    Between Life Therapist, personally trained by Dr. Michael Newton, certified Reiki
    Teacher, motivational lecturer, newspaper columnist, radio and television talk show
    host, and is currently writing another book. She has a successful practice in New
    Hampshire teaching people how to release old beliefs and self-destructive patterns to
    create powerful change and happiness for love, success and health. Dr. Erika Duffy
    holds educational seminars and does both private and telephone consultations.

Best selling author and lecturer
Author of Real Magic, Manifesting Your Destiny, Pulling
    Your Own Strings and other books.
www.waynedyer.com

Eichenbaum, Elizabeth .... Page 77
Manhattan, New York
Bachelor's Degree in psychology from New York University
Member of National Council of Geocosmic Research
A 20-year student of astrology and holistic studies.
Offers healing and empowerment to help her clients iden-
    tify and align with their true path.
Elizabeth offers in-depth, taped consultations either in person or by telephone.
212 East 83rd St. #4C
New York, NY 10028
(212)734-4928
eeichen64@hotmail.com
www.astrostrategies.com

Fine, Rebecca .... Page 35
A business owner since 1983, Rebecca Fine attributes her greatest success
    to following the principles set out by Wallace D. Wattles in his amaz-
    ing forgotten classic from 1910, The Science of Getting Rich.
Through The Science of Getting Rich Network website and her ezine, The Certain
    WayTM with tens of thousands of subscribers in 151 countries (so far!), she is
    committed to making this life-changing and very practical wisdom available to all.
She currently lives in Seattle, Washington, where she is plan-
    ning a multi-country sailing adventure for 2005.
Certain Way Productions, Inc.
350 South Center Street
Suite 500
Reno, NV 89501 USA
775-333-5949
rebeccafine@scienceofgettingrich.net

Froats, Janice .... Page 83
She is 32 years old and a single mother of 3 children ages 4, 3, and 5 weeks.
    She works for the Correctional Service of Canada as a sex offender thera-
    pist. She is in the process of opening her own life coaching business called
    Reflections of the Soul. Her purpose in life is to open people's hearts and
    help them awaken to their True and Divine selves! In addition to work-
    ing with people individually she teaches a variety of seminars including
    "Raising Spiritually Aware Children", "Discovering Your Life's Purpose",
    "Finding the Blessing in Every Crisis", and "Universal Principles".
Spiritual Teacher
Reflections of the Soul
359 Melanie Ave
Kingston, Ontario K7M 8B4
(613) 542-7171
janice.froats@sympatico.ca
www.reflectionsofthesoul.ca (under construction)

A marketing consultant and the creator of Duct Tape Marketing, a small busi-
        ness marketing system. To find more information on marketing your small
        business, visit http://www.JohnJantsch.com or the Duct Tape Marketing
        Web log at http://www.DuctTapeMarketing.com/weblog.php.
    Jantsch Communications
    201 Wyandotte, Suite 101c
    Kansas City, MO 64105
    Phone: 816-616-4151
    Fax: 816-474-4734
    john@jantschcommunications.com

    Berkley, CA
    timk@transcendentsolutions.com

    Her passion is helping others to understand, and use, all the knowledge
        she has acquired. That everyone may be inspired to seek balanced
        health, their true inner-selves and the life they dream of.
    Author of Why Wait Until You Crash? 'the' concise 'no hype' handbook to life.
    Her work includes face-to-face and telephone consultations, seminars and forums.
    'Change Your Mind and Change Your Life'
    Psychoanalyst and Health Educator
    Mentor- Information Exchange
    6 Cheriton Drive
    Riddells Creek
    Victoria Australia 3431
    www.mentoronline.com.au
    Telephone: 61-3-542-86304
    Fax: 61-3-542-86204
    jking@mentoronline.com.au

    He is retired and works from home. For extraordinary success in your life;
        health, love and prosperity, two free e-books and the following year-long
        course teach you what you can be, what health and riches you can achieve.
        The Science of Frequency Programming' entertains and Instructs, with
        all the tools of a brand new psi-evolution of positive thinking and a new
        Unified Theory of the Universe. Check it out now at: www.psi-kick.com.
    Incentive Leisure Group.SL
    C/Rio Darro, Portal 2, 20
    Urb, Molino de Viento,
    Malaga, Mijas, 29650 Spain
    0034 952591072
    tom@psi-kick.com
    www.psi-kick.com

N.D., Ph.D., Psychologist
Software Programmer for the mind: Energy Psychology Institute
Member, National Speakers Association
Publisher, www.personaltransformationpress.com
Author of seven books: Your Body Is Talking Are You Listening? 2003
Reprogramming Your Millionaire Mind 2004
Inventor of the "StressBuster"
8300 Rock Springs Rd.
Penryn, CA 95663
800-655-3846
Art@energymedicine.net
www.energymedicne.net
www.stressbuster.org

An osteopath- acupuncturist –naturopath-kinesiologist-life coach living and
working in Holywood, Northern Ireland. Through his companies, Balanced
Health Seminars and Complementary Health Ireland, he runs training groups and events, including an international convention for com-
plimentary medical practitioners. He is a keen sailor and painter, and is
especially excited by the growing field of psycho-energetic medicine.
150, High Street,
Holywood,
Co. Down BT18 9HS,
Northern Ireland, UK.
www.balancedhealthseminars.co.uk
rmccutc@aol.com
Business: 0044 2890 425953
Mobile: 0044 7876 353 339

After graduating high school he worked construction until he discovered flying. He became a private pilot then returned to college to get his com-
mercial license. He has been flying professionally for the past 29 years. In
May he turned 50 but feels like 30, and sometimes acts that young. Over
the past 10 years he has been on a more spiritual journey in his life. He
recently decided to move to Arizona and will do so later this spring.
Lghouses@earthlink.net

Wake up... Live the Life You Love, Living on Purpose

D.O.
Mother and Grandmother
Family Practice Physician
Co-author with Marie Osmond and Marcia Wilkie; New York Times Bestseller
   Behind the Smile: My Journey Out of Postpartum Depression. Author of *Healing from*
   the Heart: the Inherent Power to Heal from Within. Co-author with M. Douglas
   Moore; *First Night and Beyond: A Guide to Sexual Fulfillment for Newlyweds.*
Founder and President of the non-profit Foundation for the
   Advancement of Integrative Medicine (FAIM)
Total Health Institute
385 West 600 North
Lindon, UT 84042
801-796-8111
judimoore@tech-edge.com
Find free health information at www.faim.info

RN, CMT
She is a holistic health practitioner, although she is much more then she could ever
   explain here, in truth. She teaches Vianna Stibel's Theta Healing Technique,
   which is intentional healing and medical intuitive training. She is a cra-
   nial sacral balancing therapist, Reiki master and massage therapist. She has
   published on line at Carolyn Myss.com, "Story of the Month," titled, Oh
   God I Create My Life. She has also published an article in a local Holistic
   Newspaper called Central-Sierra Health, Resource Guide to Complementary
   Therapies for a Healthy Body, Mind, and Spirit. She is a consultant in healing, balancing and de-toxing the body with nutrition. She is also a RN super-
   visor in a busy, locked psychiatric hospital, which has helped her take who
   she is to a part of the world that may benefit greatly from the new energy.
302 South First Ave. Oakdale, Ca. 95361
209-847-6226
whitewizard156@cs.com

He was born in Buffalo, NY June 1, 1951 with no siblings, to working class parents who divorced when he was 4 yeas old. Struggled in
   school with ADD therefore, only achieved a grammar school education
   and have been a successful salesman and entrepreneur his entire life.
He has built/established 4 successful companies in the fields of direct
   mail and sales training, coaching, personal development.
All his learning and achievements have been accomplished
   through the use of books, tapes and seminars.
285-B Fairway Oaks Dr
Sedona, AZ 86351
Home: 928 284 4440
Cell: 928 254 9335
xsl2it@aol.com
www.jerrynowacki.org

MBA, CFP, LUTCF, LLIF

Arnie has been in the insurance financial services industry since 1977.
He is multi-state licensed for life and health insurance, holds a property-casualty license, and is a NASD registered representative.
He is a Certified Financial Planner, Life Underwriter Training Council Fellow, and LIMRA Leadership Institute Fellow. He has a bachelor of science degree in Business Administration, and an M.B.A. He is a member of the National Speakers Association, a frequent speaker, and trainer on both personal development and industry issues. Arnie is married, has two grown children, five grandchildren, and lives in Macedon, NY. His personal mission is to make a meaningful difference in the lives of those he comes in contact with and to allow them to make a meaningful difference in his life.

1077 Farmington Road
Macedon, NY 14502
(877) 355-7315
(315) 986-2504
arniepechler@thecertainway.com
www.thecertainway.com

CMI, CFS, DCFS, CCS
CKP Funding Services
620 Chagrin River Road
Gates Mills, OH 44040
Phone: 440-423-3466
ckpfund@ix.netcom.com
www.ckpfunding.com
www.carolynkperry.com

Senior Principal

Picard & Company; a strategic marketing and advisory firm focused on business development and customer value retention. Using his proprietary method called Relationship Architecture, he has made a career of delivering a return on a company's investment in their relationships and helping to drive growth in both small and middle market business, as well as some of the leading organizations in the world. John has been married for 25 years to his wife, Meryl, and has a daughter, Rachael, now 13. John is currently writing a book on Relationship Architecture, offering ways to drive added growth, revenue and success from marketing, without sacrificing the personal and corporate missions and values that are often the basis for customer relationships in the first place.

Picard & Company
31 Crest Drive
Murray Hill, NJ 07974
908-771-0512
Fax: 908-771-0937
jpicard@picardmarketing.com
www.picardmarketing.com

He is a medical doctor from Walsall, in the heart of England. He initially graduated with an honors degree in Economics, before a head injury prompted
him to consider a career in medicine. He went on to study at the Imperial
College School of Medicine in London, and is currently involved in setting up an innovative internet-based health service, called the "People's
Health Service", inspired by his partner Caroline's diagnosis of cancer.
thePHS
18 isis grove
willenhall
walsall west midlands WV13 1JD
United Kingdom
+0 (190) 263-4767
044 01902 634 767
www.healthradio.co.uk
rob@thephs.com
Wba2002@hotmail.com

Director of Corporate Recruiting
She has written a report and created an e-course about how to find a job by tapping
into your own personal power coupled with inside secrets from her experience
in corporate recruiting. She is also a speaker and a consultant on this topic.
195 Arizona Avenue #168
Atlanta, GA 30307
404-759-8057
jremling@t-source.com
www.ultimatejobsecrets.com

5532 Mill Creek Road
San Diego, CA 92130
office: 858-755-5595
fax: 858-755-2356
davidresnick@san.rr.com

Lorrie creates Experimental Interactive Theater and is an Engergy
Healer. She additionally writes and records songs, writes experimetn-
tal prose and poetry, and is currently producing a documentary.
www.lorrierivers.com
www.goeatworms.com
info@lorrierivers.com
803-361-2866

Wake up... Live the Life You Love, Living on Purpose

Internationally recognized author, speaker and therapist.
Master Practitioner of neurolinguistic programming, Time Line
  Therapy techniques, hypnotherapist and herbalist.
Currently, she is completing her PhD in psychology. She has assisted people
  in 11 different countries in ridding themselves of irrational fears or anxiety, as well as other issues involving negative emotions and limiting beliefs
  that may be holding them back from achieving what they want out of
  life. Roberts owns and operates a natural therapies clinic whose staff specializes in helping couples with fertility issues. In addition, Stacey's new
  programs are helping individuals eliminate emotional eating issues.
US address
6311 W North Ave
Wauwatosa, Wi 53213
Australia addresss
22 Martin St
Nerang QLD 4211
stacey@sharkeyshealingcentre.com.au
lifestrategiesunltd@hotmail.com
sharkeyshealingcentre.com.au
createoptimalhealth.com

Creator of the # 1 Best selling Wake Up...Live the Life You Love series
562-884-0062
www.wakeuplive.com

Ron Smith is a much sought after speaker, marketing consultant, coach, trainer and
  author. The title Guro (teacher) was conferred upon Ron, entrusting him to teach
  the Grandmaster's martial arts and financial arts. He is the author of the life altering "Success Mastery" series and the founder of the "Success Mastery Institute"
  as well as the "Millionaire Roundtable". Ron lives in Rancho Palos Verdes,
  CA with his wife and 7 children. For information on how you can live a more
  Powerful, Profitable and Prosperous life and to contact Ron directly, log onto:
  successmasteryinstitute.com. When the student is ready, the master will appear.

B.A. in psychology and a certified personal trainer and lifestyle & weight management consultant. George is the author of the #1 best-selling Ebook on Amazon.
com "How YOU Can Sculpt A Leaner, Healthier Body In 12 Weeks: A Guide
For Beginners!" (December 2002). The Revised version is due out in Fall 2005
and has contributions from the following experts: John Paul Catanzaro – exercise
program, Dr. Eric Serrano – nutrition, Dr. Mauro DiPasquale – supplemen-
tation). He is also the owner of Body Sculpting Corp., a company based in
Toronto, Ontario that specializes in one-stop shopping for ALL your health and
fitness needs. George's Philosophy can be summed up in his Company Slogan "A
Healthy Way To A Better Body And Mind!" President, Body Sculpting Corp.

181 Linden Avenue
Scarborough, Ontario, Canada
M1K 3J1
416-267-0856
www.bodysculpting.ca
george.stavrou@rogers.com
www.bodysculpting.ca

Inner Healing, Inc.
109 Trey Circle
Bristol, TN 37620
423-652-0233
miracles22@aol.com
innerhealing.com

Tom Tessereau is the owner and Director of the Healing Arts Center in St. Louis,
MO. With more than 30 years of study and experience in the healing arts and
sciences, he successfully combines Eastern and Western knowledge and understanding into a synthesis of bodywork, energy healing, yoga, breathwork, and
intuitive awareness. He encourages his clients and students to become an active
participant in their process of healing, guiding them back to the realization of
harmony and balance in their entire physical, emotional, mental, and spiritual
dynamic. As a transformational healer and teacher, Tom's work reflects his genu-
ine love and respect for others and their healing process. He offers his clients
and students a grace and gentleness that is a powerful and unique experience.

Healing Arts Center
2601 S. Big Bend Blvd.
St. Louis, MO 63143
Work: 314-647-8080
Toll free: 866-647-8080
Fax: 314-647-8134
tom@hacmassage.com
www.hacmassage.com

Wake up... Live the Life You Love, Living on Purpose

Brad Werner lives in Phoenix, Arizona with his wife and son. He does software consulting and computer and network training through Werner Training and Consulting, Inc. with a focus on live web-based communication. With twelve months of sunshine he enjoys desert gardening and Reiki. In addition to a technical book and several computer courses he has published a book of poetry titled Wave Particle Duality.

Werner Training and Consulting, Inc.
3867 E. Amberwood Dr.
Phoenix AZ 85048-7356
United States
Phone: 480 706-0066
Fax: 480 706-1144
brad@wernerconsulting.com
wernerconsulting.com

Since 1989, Alice Wheaton has worked with corporations throughout North America,the Pacific Rim, and Europe to provide the knowledge and skills that help them create new opportunities and close more sales.

She is inspirational, motivating and humorous presenter and the author of three books and numerous other success tools, *Say No! to Me - The True Power of Upside-Down Selling, Big Game Hunters and Closers - Attract and Keep Your Super Sellers, Cold Calling for Chickens, Cowards, and the Faint-of-Heart* and *Fear Less and Live More - Out Fox Your Fear.* Alice's latest breakthrough book, *Forgive and Forget - Strategies for Peace of Mind provides practical steps for overcoming fear and finding personal peace.*

For more information on Alice, please visit www.alicewheaton.com.
www.alicewheaton.com
awheaton@alicewheaton.com

Wake up... Live the Life You Love, Living on Purpose

Resources

Centerpointe Research Institute
1700 NW 167th Place, Suite 220
Beaverton OR 97006
800-945-2741
503-672-7117

Centerpointe Research Institute offers two programs, The Holosync Solution and The Life Principles Integration Process. The Holosync Solution uses Centerpointes proprietary Holosync audio technology to place the listener in states of deep meditation, creating dramatic and rapid changes in mental, emotional, and spiritual health. Over 150,000 people in 172 countries have used Holosync to improve their lives. By filling out a short survey at www.centerpointe.com you can get a free Holosync demo CD and a Special Report about Holosync and how it works. Or, call 800-945-2741 or 503-672-7117.

In Centerpointe's Life Principles Integration Process, you'll learn the internal processes you use to unconsciously and automatically create your internal and external results, and how to take control of this process so you can consciously and intentionally create the internal and external results you really want. For more information about The Life Principles Integration Process, and to hear a free preview lesson, visit www.centerpointe/preview.

How would you like to be in the next book
with a fabulous group of best selling authors?
Another Wake Up book is coming soon!

Visit: www.wakeuplive.com

Additional author information can be found at:

wwww.wakeupcoauthors.com/purpose

We would like to provide you with a gift
to enhance this book experience.
For your free gift, please visit

www.wakeupgift.com